"Jim Newheiser offers a wise, biblically balanced contribution to the discussion of boundaries in Christian circles and the counseling world. He affirms appropriate scriptural limits while challenging the contemporary self-centered misuse of the concept. Most especially, Dr. Newheiser calls believers to sacrificial love—even when such Christlike love means going beyond what culture or comfort deems reasonable."
 Keith A. Evans, Associate Professor of Christian
 Counseling, Reformed Theological Seminary, Charlotte

"Jim Newheiser has written an excellent book that helps us set boundaries biblically in all kinds of situations. I highly recommend this book for you and those you love."
 Charles D. Hodges Jr., Family Physician; instructor/
 counselor, Faith Biblical Counseling; editor of
 The Christian Counselor's Medical Desk Reference

"In his biblical, practical, and penetrating style, Jim Newheiser unpacks the cultural baggage around boundaries, sorts it out with God's truth, and then calls us to operate within scriptural categories bearing more resilient results. Any Christian who needs to draw clear lines in hard places will be grateful they were guided by this book!"
 Dave Harvey, President, Great Commission Collective;
 author of *The Clay Pot Conspiracy*

"This book is long overdue and much needed. With theological precision and exegetical expertise, Dr. Jim Newheiser draws on decades of counseling experience to clearly address what the Bible really says about creating boundaries in personal relationships. I highly recommend this book to anyone who wants biblical boundaries."
 John D. Street Jr., Distinguished Lecturer and Research
 Fellow in Biblical Counseling, The Master's University
 & Seminary; president, Association of Certified Biblical
 Counselors (ACBC)

"*Do I Need Boundaries?* is an engaging and timely book, answering many questions you might have about the topic from God's perspective. Dr. Newheiser differentiates between what is biblical and what is not. He explains clearly how we should think about this issue and how to respond. He also includes several case studies with thought-provoking questions. I highly recommend this resource!"
Martha Peace, Author of *The Excellent Wife*;
biblical counselor

"Relationships are wonderful, important, and complex. This is why the Bible spends so much space describing them and explaining how to navigate the challenges they pose. Jim Newheiser serves as a reliable guide to all of us who need to grow in biblical wisdom about these wonderfully complicated things we call relationships. As you read, you will encounter the teaching of a man who is marked by biblical wisdom and a desire to help you. You need to read this helpful little book."
Heath Lambert, Senior Pastor, First Baptist Church,
Jacksonville, Florida

DO I NEED BOUNDARIES?
SEEKING TO PLEASE GOD
BY LEARNING TO SAY NO

Jim Newheiser

newgrowthpress.com

New Growth Press, Greensboro, NC 27401
newgrowthpress.com
Copyright © 2025 by Jim Newheiser

All rights reserved. No part of this publication may be reproduced, stored in a retrieval system, or transmitted in any form by any means, electronic, mechanical, photocopy, recording, or otherwise, without the prior permission of the publisher, except as provided by USA copyright law.

Unless otherwise indicated, Scripture quotations are taken from The ESV® Bible (The Holy Bible, English Standard Version®). ESV® Text Edition: 2016. Copyright © 2001 by Crossway, a publishing ministry of Good News Publishers. The ESV® text has been reproduced in cooperation with and by permission of Good News Publishers. Unauthorized reproduction of this publication is prohibited. All rights reserved.

Names and identifying details have been changed in vignettes and stories shared.

Cover Design: Studio Gearbox, studiogearbox.com
Interior Typesetting/eBook: Lisa Parnell, lparnellbookservices.com

ISBN: 978-1-64507-559-2 (paperback)
ISBN: 978-1-64507-560-8 (ebook)

Library of Congress Cataloging-in-Publication Data on file

Printed in Colombia

29 28 27 26 25   1 2 3 4 5

CONTENTS

Chapter 1. Thinking Like a Christian About Boundaries 1

Chapter 2. Biblical Principles for Setting Boundaries 11

Chapter 3. Applying Biblical Principles: A Job Without Boundaries 31

Chapter 4. Applying Biblical Principles: A Child Who Comes Out as Gay or Transgender 38

Chapter 5. Applying Biblical Principles: A Single Girl Who Hopes for a Ring by Spring 43

Chapter 6. Applying Biblical Principles: In-Laws Who Act Like Outlaws 48

Chapter 7. Applying Biblical Principles: Sexual Boundaries in Marriage 54

Chapter 8. Applying Biblical Principles: Dealing with Past Abuse 60

Chapter 9. Applying Biblical Principles: Financial Boundaries 63

Chapter 10. Applying Biblical Principles: Failure to Launch 70

| Chapter 11. | Applying Biblical Principles: Addicted to Screens | 73 |

Conclusion 76

Appendix. A Biblical Perspective on Cloud and Townsend's Treatment of Boundaries............. 79

Endnotes 88

Chapter 1

THINKING LIKE A CHRISTIAN ABOUT BOUNDARIES

In the Rodgers and Hammerstein musical, *Oklahoma!*, a young woman, Ado Annie, laments in song that she is "the girl who can't say no."[1] There are many people today who can identify with Ado Annie because they find that they just can't say no to people who make inappropriate or excessive demands upon them.

Some of us have unreasonable employers who expect us to unnecessarily work long hours. Many of us deal with family members who expect us to be on call at all times, even at the last minute or if other plans have been made. Others have relatives who insist that we give financial help when asked. Perhaps we have friends and neighbors who expect help with babysitting or household projects but never offer to reciprocate. Even church leaders can burden overcommitted people, often compounding the guilt as they remind us that we are all doing it for the Lord. We all have a list of overwhelming demands that have been made on our time, money, and emotional resources.

It's true that the inability to say no can cause problems. As a wise friend stated, "When you say yes to one demand, you are saying no to others." Giving in to the tyranny of the urgent can lead to neglecting your most important God-given responsibilities. Some find themselves exhausted and overwhelmed by overcommitment. They become bitter and angry toward those who take advantage of them.

WHY PEOPLE SET BOUNDARIES

One proposed solution to this problem has been the concept of creating personal boundaries. This approach has been popular among psychologists and self-help gurus since the 1980s. People are encouraged to set limits on relationships for the sake of those individuals' own well-being. The metaphor of boundaries has become so common in popular culture that people who have never read a book about boundaries or talked to a therapist have embraced the concept and will speak of setting relationship boundaries for self-protection. You often hear people say, "I'm always doing things for others. I need to set boundaries so that I can take care of myself. I need more me time."

Although the concept of creating personal boundaries has been around for decades, the metaphor has taken on new life in our polarized culture. You may find yourself placed outside of the boundaries others have set. Individuals who make a politically (or theologically) disfavored statement on social media are often completely and permanently cut off by former friends. This behavior is now known as *canceling* people.

Tragically, families are dividing. Some young adults are convinced that they have been harmed or even traumatized by the allegedly abusive way that their parents raised them. This is not meant to diminish the terrible and very real effects of abusive parenting, but many of the abuses cited are parenting choices like expecting church attendance, enforcing curfews, and overseeing social media use. Some adult children have set strict limits on their interactions with their parents, rarely seeing them or even rarely talking or texting with them. Many have identified their parents as "toxic" and have totally cut off all contact with them. A national survey estimates that approximately 30 percent of Americans aged eighteen and older have cut off a family member.[2]

For over forty years, I have had the privilege of counseling individuals and families through many relational challenges. While it is sometimes appropriate or even necessary to say no, I am concerned that the concept of setting boundaries is being misused. In contrast, Scripture offers infallible wisdom to help us to honor God as we navigate the challenges of setting appropriate limits (boundaries) in relationships and responding to the boundaries that others set around themselves.

HOW THE BIBLE TALKS ABOUT BOUNDARIES

While therapists often use "boundaries" in a metaphorical sense for setting limits on relationships, in the Bible, boundaries are usually literal physical borders between political entities (Numbers 35:26–28, 32; Joshua 13:23, 27; 15:1–2; Judges 2:9; Proverbs 15:25; Ezekiel 45:1–7; Acts 17:26; etc.). There are times in Scripture where physical boundaries or limitations have spiritual implications. The fruit of the tree of the knowledge of good and evil was off-limits for the first man and woman (Genesis 2:17), and there were dire consequences for the violation of that "boundary."

Throughout the Bible we are called to set limits (or boundaries) on our behavior. God's law, including the

Ten Commandments, puts sins such as disrespect of parents, murder, adultery, stealing, and lying off-limits. Children need limits or both they and their parents will suffer (Proverbs 29:15).

In the Bible, boundaries distinguish one thing from another—one person's land from someone else's, sin from righteousness, the holy from the unholy, the permissible from the impermissible, Christians from unbelievers. Boundaries are a necessary fact of life; we can't live without them. All people, everywhere, have boundaries. How we differ is in where we draw the boundaries. God's boundaries are always good, and transgressing them comes with consequences.

This quick look at what Scripture says about boundaries might seem pretty far removed from how we use the term in contemporary culture. But the issues that "boundary setting" deals with are addressed all through the Bible. God has much to say about how we relate to others, whether we should say no or yes, and how we should use our time. Sadly, much of the discussion on "setting boundaries" in personal relationships centers on what's best for the person who is setting the boundary. But Christians have a different starting point. Their goal is to live a life pleasing to God (Ephesians 5:8–10). Starting there will give you clear directions on difficult relationships and difficult decisions.

PLEASING GOD, NOT PEOPLE, GIVES DIRECTIONS ON SETTING BOUNDARIES

The most important thing to remember is that the solution to these problems is not going from pleasing others (Galatians 1:10) to pleasing yourself (2 Timothy 3:2). Instead, our great aim should be to please God (2 Corinthians 5:9).

CAN ALL (OR EVEN MOST) RELATIONSHIP PROBLEMS BE SOLVED BY SETTING APPROPRIATE BOUNDARIES?

If you read popular books on boundaries, like *Boundaries: When to Say Yes, How to Say No to Take Control of Your Life*, by Dr. Henry Cloud and Dr. John Townsend,[3] you will notice that they teach that most interpersonal problems and conflicts would be solved by setting the right relational boundaries. Cloud and Townsend begin their book with a description of a day in the boundaryless life of Sherrie. She is overwhelmed by the demands and expectations of others, including her children's school, her needy mother, her irresponsible coworkers, her unreasonable boss, her selfish friends, her unhelpful children, her unsupportive husband, and even her insensitive church leaders. She lives in fear of disappointing others. She is exhausted, tempted to bitterness, and worried that important relationships are falling apart.

The book concludes with a day in Sherrie's new, better life, in which her boundaries have been firmly established according to the principles advocated by the authors. Sherrie wisely and appropriately handles every inappropriate imposition. She has a support group. Her family members are pulling their own weight. She is in a church which respects boundaries. She no longer does tasks for her irresponsible coworkers, and she has even received a job promotion from her employer. Her husband is no longer grumpy, and her marriage has greatly improved. People are no longer taking advantage of her. All is well.

At first glance, it might seem that this book is positive—we would all like a simple, easy-to-follow solution to problems and conflict with others. But while Cloud and

Townsend do well at describing the problem, they fall short of biblical standards in their interpretation of the problem and in establishing a biblical, gospel-centered solution (see the appendix on p. 79 for an in-depth review of their book).

The popular discussions of boundary setting promise that our problems, too, will be solved by setting proper boundaries. But Scripture teaches that our problems are deeper than our relationships and that the solutions are more complex than merely establishing relational limits. While relationships take wisdom, our deepest problem is that "all we like sheep have gone astray; we have turned—every one—to his own way." And Jesus provides the solution to our wayward hearts: "and the Lord has laid on him the iniquity of us all" (Isaiah 53:6). When we turn from our own ways and to Jesus in faith, then he gives us his Spirit to counsel, comfort, convict, and guide (John 14:26; 16:8–14).

DON'T REPLACE THE GOAL OF PLEASING OTHERS WITH THE GOAL OF PLEASING YOURSELF

The usual advice given about boundaries focuses on how we will benefit by requiring others to respect our limits. This approach to setting boundaries can lead people to replace their goal of pleasing others with a new goal of pleasing themselves. Scripture teaches that our most important relationship is with God and that we should embrace his control of every aspect of our lives, including our relationships, as our chief aim is not to protect and please ourselves but instead to please him: "'God opposes the proud but gives grace to the humble.' Submit yourselves therefore to God" (James 4:6–7).

This unbiblical approach to our relational problems encourages us to think we can solve our own problems. But it isn't that simple. Sin affects both our relationships with God and our relationships with one another. We can't fix our relationships by our efforts or imposing our morality on others. We all need the gospel of Christ. Christ is the one who died not only to reconcile us with God but also to help us be graciously reconciled to one another (Ephesians 4:31–5:2).

While Cloud, Townsend, and others like them address a real problem (that people who can't say no can become overcommitted and overwhelmed), their interpretation of the problem is flawed, and their proposed solution is inadequate. As we shall see, there is a better way.

A DEEPER (AND BIBLICAL) LOOK AT OUR MOTIVATION FOR SAYING YES OR NO

What are the inward heart motivations of overcommitted, overwhelmed people? Why do we allow others to control us and use us? The Bible gives us insight into the root of the problem when it says, "The fear of man lays a snare" (Proverbs 29:25a).

What is happening in our hearts when we are constantly saying yes to the demands that others make? Ed Welch comments on the effect of following the modern teachings on boundary setting when he writes,

> The other-oriented command to love is revised so that it becomes a self-oriented goal to never disappoint, to always have people pleased with you, to never have conflict . . . Is the emphasis on loving another person or is it on being loved by another

person? . . . The goal of followers of Christ is to love others more than need love from others. Does being loved by this person become the center of your life, replacing God Himself?[4]

Remember that when we say yes to one demand, we are by implication saying no to other demands. Being a people pleaser means we are more concerned about saying yes to demanding people so that they approve of us than saying yes to God and doing what pleases him. Putting anything (including other people) ahead of God means that we are not worshipping and loving God. The Bible calls this idolatry—and the consequences of idolatry hurt us and others.

The Bible says that people pleasers are caught like an animal in a trap—"The fear of man lays a snare" (Proverbs 29:25). Jeremiah 17:5–6 describes those who make other people more important than God as being under a curse:

> Thus says the LORD: "Cursed is the man who trusts in man and makes flesh his strength, whose heart turns away from the LORD. He is like a shrub in the desert, and shall not see any good come. He shall dwell in the parched places of the wilderness, in an uninhabited salt land."

Have you noticed that when we make it our aim to please others, we often feel dry, like a dying bush in a dry desert?

HOW CAN WE SET APPROPRIATE BOUNDARIES?

The solution proposed by many psychologists to the problem of boundary violations is to "take control of your life."

The result is that those who have been overwhelmed by the expectations of other people often go from making other people the center of their lives to making themselves the center of their lives. But moving from pleasing others to pleasing self will not solve the problem.

When you think about the problem of saying no in your life, isn't it freeing to flip the script from choosing to either please others or please yourself to choosing to please God? Replacing wanting to make others happy with wanting to make ourselves happy is not the way to the blessed life. Instead, following Jesus and living for him will give us freedom in our relationships—even when we have disappointed people. This is what it means to be a Christian. Paul puts it like this: "For am I now seeking the approval of man, or of God? Or am I trying to please man? If I were still trying to please man, I would not be a servant of Christ" (Galatians 1:10).

The "take control of your life" solution does not address the heart issues that make us susceptible to having our lives controlled by the demands of others, nor does it help us live in a way that pleases and honors God. Those who struggle with boundaries due to underlying issues like bad theology (*God will only love me if I treat others perfectly*), scriptural abuse (when others twist Scripture to make us do what they want), lack of reflection (thinking, *I'm just too busy to think about why I'm always saying yes*), or other faulty functional beliefs will not have the opportunity to identify these underlying issues.

The Bible offers the God-centered alternative. We repent of pleasing others, and we devote ourselves to pleasing God in all things—including our relationships and the demands they make. Proverbs 29:25 tells us how we can escape the snare set by the fear of man: "But whoever trusts in the Lord is safe." Instead of worrying about what others think of us, we set our focus on following God's ways.

The antidote to the dryness experienced by those who make people too important is that they should grow in trusting the Lord; then they will flourish:

> "Blessed is the man who trusts in the Lord, whose trust is the Lord. He is like a tree planted by water, that sends out its roots by the stream, and does not fear when heat comes, for its leaves remain green, and is not anxious in the year of drought, for it does not cease to bear fruit." (Jeremiah 17:7–8)

Trust in the Lord is not merely a feeling. When we are convinced that he is good and that his ways are best, we actively seek to please and obey him, so we flourish. This does not mean that life will always be trouble-free, but even hardship, or what Jesus calls "pruning" (John 15:2), is for our good (Romans 8:28).

QUESTIONS FOR REFLECTION

1. How does the concept of boundaries in the Bible differ from how psychologists speak of boundaries?

2. Given that the Bible uses the word *boundaries* in a literal sense, is there any risk to claiming biblical warrant for using the term metaphorically?

3. What are some of the reasons you struggle to set reasonable boundaries?

Chapter 2

BIBLICAL PRINCIPLES FOR SETTING BOUNDARIES

Tiana has a demanding boss who expects her to be on call whenever she is needed. Tiana is afraid of losing her job and doesn't like conflict, but she is also tired and overwhelmed. She doesn't know what to do.

Nate's pastor relies on him for a lot of help. He asks him to counsel needy people and head up various committees. When Nate says he needs to spend time with his family, his pastor tells him that his church should be his priority. Nate feels guilty that he isn't putting God first. He doesn't know what to do.

Emma says yes to the many requests that come her way—her teenagers need a ride, her neighbors' kids need babysitting, her boss has an important project she has to attend to right away, and her husband wants her to work less and spend more time with him. She feels like she is being pulled in too many directions and doesn't know how she will be able to keep going.

Tiana, Nate, and Emma all need help in setting relational limits (or boundaries). You probably need help too!

What is God's way forward in all these hard-to-figure-out scenarios?

When others ask hard things of us, how can we decide what to do? It would bring a great deal of clarity to many of our complex situations if we took a step back and remembered the big picture. Jesus summed up the entire Law in two memorable commands—they infallibly point the right way forward.

OUR CHIEF AIM IS TO LOVE AND PLEASE GOD

When asked which commandment is the most important commandment, Jesus answered, "The most important is, 'Hear, O Israel: The Lord our God, the Lord is one. And you shall love the Lord your God with all your heart and with all your soul and with all your mind and with all your strength'" (Mark 12:29–30). A friend of mine calls Paul's words in 2 Corinthians 5:9 our "Prime Directive" (some will appreciate the *Star Trek* reference), the principle that should govern all our choices: "So whether we are at home or away, we make it our aim to please him."

Many of our decisions would be simplified if we kept this question in the forefront of our minds: What would please God? We know the will of God through his infallible and all-sufficient Word, which equips us for every good work (2 Timothy 3:16–17). Submit to God and allow *him* to take control of your life.

There will be times when we must say no to people because of our allegiance to God. When Potiphar's wife attempted to seduce Joseph, he said, "How then can I do this great wickedness and sin against God?" (Genesis 39:9b). When told to stop preaching the gospel, "Peter and the apostles answered, 'We must obey God rather than men'" (Acts 5:29). Eli was rebuked and ultimately lost everything because he honored his sons above God (1 Samuel 2:29–34). In each of these cases, God's people were called to make God-pleasing choices which would displease others.

Jesus warned that we would face situations in which our love for God would be tested by the demands of others, including family members:

> "Do you think that I have come to give peace on earth? No, I tell you, but rather division. For from now on in one house there will be five divided, three against two and two against three. They will be divided, father against son and son against father, mother against daughter and daughter against mother, mother-in-law against her daughter-in-law and daughter-in-law against mother-in-law." (Luke 12:51–53)

He also warned, "If anyone comes to me and does not hate his own father and mother and wife and children and brothers and sisters, yes, and even his own life, he cannot be my disciple" (Luke 14:26). When we experience a conflict between what God wants from us and what others demand, we must put our loyalty to the Lord first, even above our families.

OUR SECOND PRIORITY IS TO LOVE OTHERS

After declaring the greatest commandment, Jesus went on to say, "The second is this: 'You shall love your neighbor as yourself.' There is no other commandment greater than these" (Mark 12:31). As we seek to wisely love others, we need wisdom from the Word and help from the Spirit. The example of Jesus is our best guide.

Rather than merely viewing ourselves as individuals whose rights must be protected inside of our personal boundaries, we are to recall that we are members of the communities (especially our families and churches) in which God has placed us. Christians should think in terms of "we," not merely "I." The Lord's Prayer begins not with "my Father" but "our Father." Scripture calls us to be selfless servants who follow in the steps of Christ by sacrificially loving others. After washing his disciples' feet, Jesus declared,

> "You call me Teacher and Lord, and you are right, for so I am. If I then, your Lord and Teacher, have washed your feet, you also ought to wash one another's feet. For I have given you an example, that you also should do just as I have done to you." (John 13:13–15)

There will be times when we ought to set aside our own desires and preferences to humbly care for others:

> Do nothing from selfish ambition or conceit, but in humility count others more significant than yourselves. Let each of you look not only to his own interests, but also to the interests of others. Have this mind among yourselves, which is yours in Christ Jesus. (Philippians 2:3–5)

Within the church (and our families), we will have the opportunity to patiently bear with the sins and weaknesses of others. When people wrong us, we are called to respond in love: "Above all, keep loving one another earnestly, since love covers a multitude of sins" (1 Peter 4:8). Our communities include some awkward, needy people for whom we are called to care as we follow in the steps of Jesus:

> We who are strong have an obligation to bear with the failings of the weak, and not to please ourselves. Let each of us please his neighbor for his good, to build him up. For Christ did not please himself, but as it is written, "The reproaches of those who reproached you fell on me." (Romans 15:1–3)

This does not mean that Scripture teaches that we should allow ourselves to be controlled by every demand others make. Sometimes the most loving and wise thing we can do is say no. For example, Paul says that the church should not offer financial assistance to those who are unwilling to work (2 Thessalonians 3:10–12). Helping them would simply continue to enable their sin and would be bad stewardship of the Lord's resources. Their financial need may drive them to work: "A worker's appetite works for him; his mouth urges him on" (Proverbs 16:26).

Often loving others means that we must admonish or correct them: "Faithful are the wounds of a friend" (Proverbs 27:6a). Scripture tells us when and how to bring correction:

> Brothers, if anyone is caught in any transgression, you who are spiritual should restore him in a spirit of gentleness. Keep watch on yourself, lest you too be tempted. Bear one another's burdens, and so fulfill the law of Christ. (Galatians 6:1–2)

Some of us are conflict avoiders—often because of our wrong bent to be people pleasers. Failing to confront the sins of others can displease God and harm those who need correction: "You shall not hate your brother in your heart, but you shall reason frankly with your neighbor, lest you incur sin because of him" (Leviticus 19:17). The way to overcome conflict avoidance is to focus upon pleasing God by doing what God calls you to do in a particular situation.

SET BOUNDARIES BASED UPON BIBLICAL PRINCIPLES

We will sometimes face situations in which we wonder whether we should sacrificially accommodate the expectations of those who are weak or whether it would be wiser and more loving to say no. We all have God-given responsibilities. Rather than being controlled by the tyranny of the demands of others, we can learn to be intentional about establishing priorities in every sphere of life. Ask God for wisdom when facing such challenges (James 1:5). The biblical considerations below should help you to discern which course would please God in challenging circumstances.

Consider what the Bible says about various relationships

The Bible has a great deal to say about our specific responsibilities in various kinds of relationships: employer-employee, husband-wife, government official-citizen, parent-child, rich person-poor person, elder-church member, neighbor-neighbor, sibling-sibling, and friend-friend. In addition to direct commands, the Bible also provides a great deal of wisdom that can provide insight into how to navigate these relationships well. To draw appropriate boundaries in all these relationships, we need to start by taking in the whole counsel of God.

Recognize that some boundaries are necessary to keep us safe

One of the main categories of relationships around which we need to set boundaries are relationships with people who endanger us physically or spiritually. We also must be on guard against manipulation and allowing other people's desires, rather than obedience to the two greatest commandments, to drive our decision-making.

For example, Sue's husband, Dave, often indulges in outbursts of anger in which he grabs her or blocks her from getting away from him. Once he raised a fist and threatened to "give her what she deserves" for her alleged disrespect. While he hasn't yet caused physical harm to the children, Dave often yells at them in anger. Sue is worried about how the children could be harmed physically or emotionally. Sue is also confused because her husband quotes scriptural passages such as Ephesians 5:22, "Wives, submit to your own husbands, as to the Lord," as the reason that she should quietly subject herself to his mistreatment. When Sue sought counsel from church leaders, they unhelpfully told her to remain quiet and pray that Dave would change. They quoted 1 Peter 3:1–2, "Likewise, wives, be subject to your own husbands, so that even if some do not obey the word, they may be won without a word by the conduct of their wives, when they see your respectful and pure conduct." They told her that if she would do a better job of loving her husband, he would change.

But the biblical call to love others does not mean that we must submit to abuse or endanger ourselves. "The prudent sees danger and hides himself" (Proverbs 22:3a). Passages which speak of a wife's submission to her husband (Ephesians 5:22–24) and children obeying their parents (Ephesians 6:1–3) are sometimes misused to force victims of abuse to remain in circumstances where they are being mistreated.

However, Scripture contains many examples of righteous people justifiably fleeing from those who would harm them. In some of these cases, the oppressors from whom they are escaping are in positions of authority (Acts 8:1; 9:1–2). David takes drastic measures to escape from King Saul who seeks to kill him (1 Samuel 18:11; 23:1–27:12). The apostle Paul, by being lowered through a hole in the city wall in Damascus, escapes the Jews who are trying to murder him (Acts 9:23–25). There are occasions in the life of our Lord Jesus when he escapes those who seek to kill him before his time (Matthew 2:13–15a; John 10:39). In the same way, Jesus's followers, including women like Sue, are free to escape those who would harm or oppress them. The danger we might need to escape from isn't always physical. Hateful or threatening words can also be very destructive: "With his mouth the godless man would destroy his neighbor" (Proverbs 11:9a).

I must add a word of caution, however. The concepts of safety, danger, hate, and harm have been expanded in recent years. Some claim that speech promoting ideas they find offensive, such as biblical teaching on gender and marriage, is violent and must be suppressed. They say that people who hold such disfavored views are toxic, narcissistic, and unsafe. This expanded view of harm has been used in workplaces and in educational environments to silence or even punish those who don't agree with unbiblical ideas. This approach has also been used as an excuse to totally "cancel" dangerous family members or for spouses to unjustifiably separate or divorce, thus sadly and unnecessarily leading to complete estrangement. When the harm is not physical, proceed carefully and obtain an abundance of wise counsel.

Avoid those who have a bad spiritual influence on you

Lexi, a recent college graduate, had also recently come to faith in Christ and was being discipled by an older woman at her church. During college, Lexi had a group of close female friends who would go out bar hopping and partying on the weekends, often hooking up with guys. Lexi hoped that she would be able to share her new faith with her friends, but she found that when she went out with them, she would drink too much, and at one recent party, she found herself in a sinfully compromising position with a man she had just met.

Her mentor encouraged her to memorize Proverbs 13:20: "Whoever walks with the wise becomes wise, but the companion of fools will suffer harm." Scripture contains many warnings about how ungodly companions can have a very negative influence on Christians: "Do not be deceived: 'Bad company ruins good morals'" (1 Corinthians 15:33). Lexi's mentor said that there are times when we must separate ourselves from those who engage in ungodly practices and encourage us to join them (Proverbs 23:20; 2 Timothy 3:5). The apostle Paul likens the risk we face from being influenced by ungodly peers to the danger the pagan nations posed to Israel under the old covenant:

> Do not be unequally yoked with unbelievers. For what partnership has righteousness with lawlessness? Or what fellowship has light with darkness? What accord has Christ with Belial? Or what portion does a believer share with an unbeliever? What agreement has the temple of God with idols? For we are the temple of the living God; as God said, "I will make my dwelling among them and walk among them, and I will be their God, and they shall be my people. Therefore go out from their midst, and be separate from them, says the Lord, and touch no unclean thing; then I will welcome you, and I will be a father to you, and you shall be sons and daughters to me, says the Lord Almighty." (2 Corinthians 6:14–18)

Coming to faith in Christ means that we are no longer part of the world that is in rebellion against God and enslaved to sin: "He has delivered us from the domain of darkness and transferred us to the kingdom of his beloved Son, in whom we have redemption, the forgiveness of sins" (Colossians 1:13–14). Lexi's former friends may not understand why she no longer joins them. They may reject or insult her. Such was the experience of the first Christians:

> For the time that is past suffices for doing what the Gentiles want to do, living in sensuality, passions, drunkenness, orgies, drinking parties, and lawless idolatry. With respect to this they are surprised when you do not join them in the same flood of debauchery, and they malign you. (1 Peter 4:3–4)

While Lexi may desire to have some contact with her former friends with the hope of sharing the gospel with them, she realizes that she can no longer join them in her former lifestyle. She can't allow herself to be with them in situations in which they are more likely to be a bad influence on her than she is to be a good influence on them. When her former companions question why Lexi no longer joins them, she may have an opportunity to share with them the new life she has in Christ. Lexi should pursue close relationships with people in her new community, the church. They, the wise (Proverbs 13:20a), will help her to resist temptation and to grow in wisdom and holiness (Hebrews 3:13; 10:24–25).

Don't allow yourself to be manipulated

Some people are aggressive and intrusive when trying to get you to meet their demands. They may try to manipulate you with anger, guilt, and/or flattery (Proverbs 29:5). You need to be prepared to disappoint them. Use discernment when evaluating the urgency of a particular request. Some people try to "jump the line" by texting or calling with an "urgent" request. "Urgent" requests must be evaluated according to our understanding of the priorities God has given us. I have a counselee who will text or call and say, "Could I have five minutes of your time?" I realize that if I respond, I will lose at least forty-five minutes of my day. It would be poor stewardship of my time to interrupt family time or important work every time his text comes in.

BE PREPARED TO ENFORCE YOUR BOUNDARIES

Simply drawing boundaries doesn't always result in people respecting our boundaries. So, what do you do when people try to cross a boundary you draw? If you give in to their demands, they will continue to violate the limits you tried to set. You must maintain your focus on pleasing God and loving others well, which means that sometimes you must say no! How can you do that? Here are some biblical ways of thinking through these issues.

Wisely and intentionally set boundaries on your time

One of the most important areas we will all need to set boundaries in is time management. Doing this well requires facing our limitations and planning intentionally. But to know how to plan our time in a way that shows love for God and love for others while also respecting our limitations, we will have to consider biblical categories like calling, season of life, remembering that it's not all dependent on us, recognizing which activities have greater and lesser importance, and being willing to say no to good opportunities so we can say yes to the most important opportunities. What are some things to consider?

Face your limitations. You are finite—you can't say yes to everyone and everything. Even Jesus experienced the limitations of his human nature. He needed food and rest. He couldn't be everywhere simultaneously. He required time alone with the Father (Matthew 14:23). He didn't meet every demand people made of him. He limited the number of his close friends. Rather than being controlled by the tyranny of the demands of others, we must be intentional about establishing priorities in every sphere of life.

Plan your time. Proverbs 21:5 is one of my favorite verses: "The plans of the diligent lead surely to abundance, but everyone who is hasty comes only to poverty." You reflect your financial priorities through making and using a budget. Those who don't plan often waste money on things that are less important and then run out of money. In the same way, it is important that you budget and plan your time to reflect your commitment to the priorities God has given you. You need time to read God's Word and to pray. You need sufficient rest and exercise. You need to fulfill your responsibilities to your family, your vocation, and your church. Failure to plan leads to poverty, both in finances and in time. I talk with those close to me about how I should be using my time and then use my calendar to plan time according to my sense of God's calling on my life. Being able to talk with other Christians you trust about these issues is an important way to get God's perspective on your daily decisions about what to spend your time on.

Consider your calling. When someone has an expectation of you, a good question to ask is, "What claim does this person have on my time?" When Sanballat and Geshem sent a message asking Nehemiah to meet with them, Nehemiah responded by saying that his calling from God to rebuild the wall of Jerusalem couldn't be interrupted: "And I sent messengers to them, saying, 'I am doing a great work and I cannot come down. Why should the work stop while I leave it and come down to you?'" (Nehemiah 6:3).

Jesus also had priorities in his ministry: "He answered, 'I was sent only to the lost sheep of the house of Israel'" (Matthew 15:24). Yet he said that as he responded to the Canaanite woman's humble plea that even the dogs feed on the crumbs which fall from their master's table (Matthew 15:27–28). Jesus shows us the way to not only express our priorities but also to be willing to set them aside when we see a pressing need. Once, when I was rushing into the church building to be on time for prayer with the elders in my church, I saw an elderly man who suffered from dementia standing outside looking lost. While I value being on time, in that moment, my priority changed to caring for this man.

On the other hand, I counseled a man who complained that when he had called to make an appointment with the pastor of the megachurch he sometimes attended, he was told that the senior pastor was unavailable, but that another pastor could meet with him. The senior pastor recognized that his calling from God precluded him from meeting with every person who requested an hour. God has given each of us various responsibilities including our work, our church, our spouses, our children, and our extended families. While it may be difficult to know precisely how we should allocate our time and energy, we should take a moment to be deliberate rather than being tossed by the winds of the expectations and demands of others. As you contemplate your priorities and your calling, seek counsel from those who know you best and who know the Scriptures well (Proverbs 11:14).

Consider your present season of life. Paul, encouraging the Corinthians to consider the benefits of being single, illustrates that people in different situations have different demands on their time:

> I want you to be free from anxieties. The unmarried man is anxious about the things of the Lord, how to please the Lord. But the married man is anxious about worldly things, how to please his wife, and his interests are divided. And the unmarried or betrothed woman is anxious about the things of

the Lord, how to be holy in body and spirit. But the married woman is anxious about worldly things, how to please her husband. (1 Corinthians 7:32–34)

Those who are single, whether for a season or for life, generally have much more flexibility with their time than those who are married. Those who are married with small children in the home usually have less flexibility with their time than those whose nests have emptied. Those who are in their seventies will have less energy than those who are in their thirties. A man who is helping his wife raise their children should not feel guilty because he can't do as much for the church as he used to when he was single or what he expects to do in the future when his kids are out of the house. His commitment to his family may also mean that he should limit how many hours he devotes to his vocation and how much he travels, even if this means that he might be passed over for promotion. The young woman with children may not have as much time to mentor other women as she hopes to in the future when she is older (Titus 2:3–5).

When my wife, Caroline, homeschooled our three sons, she was limited in the time she could commit to church ministries. After our children were grown, she became certified as a biblical counselor, completed her master's degree in biblical counseling, and started training and counseling women as a vocation. We should consider our current season in life as we set our priorities so that we do not neglect our God-given responsibilities, particularly in terms of our familial obligations, such as caring for young children or aging parents. The invisible and often thankless nature of this labor can tempt us to deprioritize it, but God makes it clear in multiple passages that caring for our families should be high on our list of priorities.

Don't believe the lie that everything depends upon you

One cause of overcommitment comes from our proud belief that the world will fall apart if we don't do everything asked of us. Sometimes people who ask us for help make it sound as if we are the only ones who can help them and that we need to get involved immediately. It can be flattering to be told that you are indispensable. But remember that "A man who flatters his neighbor spreads a net for his feet" (Proverbs 29:5).

We must not overestimate our own importance or underestimate the gifts God has given to others in the church body. We must trust that God will accomplish his good purposes even if we can't do it all. Sometimes we need to actively delegate. Often, we should get out of the way so that others can use their gifts and do their part. A biblical example of the principle of letting others share the burden can be found in Exodus, where Moses was constantly acting as a judge in cases between the people (Exodus 18:13–16). Seeing this, Moses's father-in-law Jethro said to him:

> Look for able men from all the people, men who fear God, who are trustworthy and hate a bribe, and place such men over the people as chiefs of thousands, of hundreds, of fifties, and of tens. And let them judge the people at all times. Every great matter they shall bring to you, but any small matter they shall decide themselves. So it will be

easier for you, and they will bear the burden with you. If you do this, God will direct you, you will be able to endure, and all this people also will go to their place in peace. (Exodus 18:21–23)

Some of us need to heed Jethro's wise counsel.

Don't let less important pursuits crowd out what is crucial

We all enjoy activities that are not necessary but can be stress relieving or relaxing. Some enjoy catching up with friends by looking at social media. Some get a thrill out of playing video games (though I can't understand why). Some love to play sports or engage in hobbies. Some de-stress by watching sports or old movies. Many are entertained by going to concerts. We can't say that any of these activities are sinful in and of themselves. But any of them can become so life dominating that we neglect more important things. Think, for example, of the husband who rushes past his wife and kids when he gets home so that he can watch sports or play his new video game, or think of the people who spend hours scrolling through Facebook or Instagram and then realize that their day has been unproductive.

I have always enjoyed running. I also learned that running could become addictive and life dominating. I saw people whose entire lives revolved around their workouts and races. So I sought to impose some limits on my devotion to running. When our children were still in the house, I never ran for more than an hour a day because I was needed at home. I also decided not to force family activities to fit around my running schedule, nor to let running races keep me from church on the Lord's Day. After the children were fully grown, I had time to train for running longer distances.

There are many other good activities that can crowd out what is most important. The demands of children's activities, such as competitive soccer, dance, and drama, can dominate an entire family for months at a time. Sometimes we will have to choose to say no (and perhaps face the anger or disappointment of others) to fulfill what we understand to be the most important things to which God calls us. Paul expresses this well: "'All things are lawful for me,' but not all things are helpful. 'All things are lawful for me,' but I will not be dominated by anything" (1 Corinthians 6:12). An important practical step is being intentional about setting boundaries on the time we will spend on activities such as social media, hobbies, entertainment, and children's activities. Parents of teens would be wise to set specific limits on their screen time, including video games and social media, and gradually help them become more independent in setting wise boundaries in these areas.

Sometimes saying yes to the most important thing means saying no to a good thing

The apostle Paul records a fascinating choice he once made:

> When I came to Troas to preach the gospel of Christ, even though a door was opened for me in the Lord, my spirit was not at rest because I did not find my brother Titus there. So I took leave of them and went on to Macedonia. (2 Corinthians 2:12–13)

Paul had a good opportunity for ministry in Troas, but he concluded that the Lord had given him a more important priority, so he left for Macedonia. We sometimes will have to choose one of many good situations into which we could invest our time and energy.

In addition to our work teaching and mentoring future church leaders at Reformed Theological Seminary in Charlotte, my wife and I do a limited amount of biblical counseling. There are far more people who want to be counseled than we have time and strength to manage. So, we must set a limit to the number of cases we can counsel so that we will not neglect our primary responsibility to equip future church leaders at the seminary. Even further, we have set priorities among those seeking our counsel. Our first priority is to work with students and their wives since they are our primary ministry responsibility. We also give high priority to the needs of our local church, where I serve as an elder. Next, we give priority to pastors, missionaries, and their families because so many are affected if those groups of people are in crisis. Then we take counselees who will allow students to observe their sessions because these cases help us to achieve our primary task of educating and equipping. It is hard to maintain these priorities when people who are in need come pleading for help. It would be good to care for them all, but, in many cases, helping them would result in neglecting higher-priority responsibilities God has given to us. We must trust the Lord to meet their needs.

CONCLUSION

Some of the most difficult boundaries we will need to set will involve deciding between two good things, or, in other cases, rightly prioritizing our obedience to two different biblical commands such as serving in church and caring for our families. We must give careful thought to these matters, seek out wise counselors, pray for wisdom, and then draw clear boundaries so that instead of being manipulated or driven by the tyranny of the urgent, we will obey the command to make "the best use of the time" (Colossians 4:5; Ephesians 5:16).

QUESTIONS FOR REFLECTION

1. How do you know when it is right to make sacrifices to please someone else as opposed to when it would be wrong to do so?

2. What are legitimate reasons to distance yourself from someone?

3. After reading through this chapter, are there any boundaries you realized you need to set or change to love God and love others?

Chapter 3

APPLYING BIBLICAL PRINCIPLES: A JOB WITHOUT BOUNDARIES

Real life can be quite messy, and sometimes the path forward feels very murky indeed. In the remaining chapters of this book, we will look at a number of case studies where you can practice applying the biblical principles discussed in chapter 2. Even if your particular circumstances are not described, the goal is that, with practice, you will grow in wisdom as you see how these principles play out in real-life scenarios. I have changed names and details in these stories, but they are based on my interactions with real people. As you read through the case studies, consider how you would apply the biblical principles discussed previously to draw wise boundaries. The first case study is about a couple who is impacted by the husband's job, which seems to have no boundaries.

MY JOB WITHOUT BOUNDARIES

When I worked for an oil company during my twenties, I sometimes had to work overtime, but when I left the office,

I was done for the day and didn't have to think about my job until the next morning. When I entered full-time ministry, I quickly realized that I was never "done." Counseling sessions and meetings often took place during evenings and weekends because that was when others were available. Even if I didn't have a meeting scheduled, there was always one more call I could make, one more email I could write, one more pastoral visit I could schedule, and one more commentary I could consult for my sermon manuscript. Furthermore, from the standpoint of many church members, I was always on call. Sometimes people would drop by unannounced. My phone could ring at any hour, day or night—sometimes because of a crisis such as a medical emergency or a death, sometimes because of a counseling emergency. For example, I once received a late-night call from a wife who had just learned that her husband was having an affair. But sometimes less urgent ministry demands would intrude upon family responsibilities and rest. Like the dinnertime text, "Pastor, how much should we pay the guest speaker for the women's retreat? Our committee can't agree." I needed to protect the time for important things like spending time with my wife and my children.

Caroline and I often counsel ministry couples whose marriages are in crisis. A very frequent problem is that the wife is upset because her husband has neglected her and the children due to ministry responsibilities. Some pastors are so conscientious about their calling that they think they must immediately answer every text and phone call, even if it is dinnertime, and that they must respond to every email within minutes. Planned family time is frequently interrupted by a pastoral "emergency." If the pastor's wife complains about his lack of attention to the family, she is made to feel guilty for selfishly pulling her husband away from the Lord's work. Some wives, after many years of neglect, have become extremely embittered. Some have even threatened divorce.

PASTOR JOHN AND HIS WIFE JENNY

Pastor John and his wife Jenny were referred to us for counseling. John had been a straight-A student and served as the research assistant for a renowned professor while in seminary. During their seminary years, Jenny was troubled when John would study late into the night and during weekends, but she looked forward to the day when they would be settled in a church and life could return to normal. Sadly, their married life didn't improve after seminary. John was a perfectionist who spent at least sixty hours a week preparing his sermons for Sunday morning, Sunday evening, and Wednesday night. In addition, he had committee meetings at least two nights a week and spent hours each day meeting with church members in person or over the phone.

Jenny tried to be supportive by opening their home in hospitality, leading the women's ministry, participating in the worship team, and planning all church social events. Sometimes when Jenny complained about John's lack of attention to their marriage, he planned a date night, but some of these were canceled at the last minute because someone in the church "needed" John. When they did finally go on a date, John kept looking at his phone while Jenny fought her annoyance. Once, while they were out together, John got up from their dinner and rushed out the door because he had received what he deemed to be an "urgent" text. Jenny felt that she was at her limit, so to get John's attention, Jenny packed up and went for an extended visit with her parents, who lived in another state. Take a moment and consider: What are the boundaries John needed to place around his job to best love God and love others? What are some of the principles discussed in chapter 3 that could guide his decision-making here?

When they came to us for counseling, we shared with John that, as devoted as he was to the ministry, he would not be qualified to serve God as a pastor/elder if his marriage and home were not in good order (1 Timothy 3:2–5). As a married man, he can't use his service to the Lord as an excuse for neglecting his wife. Paul tells us that when a man marries, he cannot live as if he is single, ignoring his wife for the sake of the ministry: "The married man is anxious about worldly things, how to please his wife" (1 Corinthians 7:33). John was confused about how to balance his calling as a pastor and an elder with his calling to love his wife and his family. We helped John by sharing with him that the Bible does not teach that marriage is an inferior state for ministers of the gospel. Most of us will be more fit for God's service as married men. But to fulfill his calling to his marriage and family, a pastor may not be able to do everything that a single man can do.

For John to think biblically about his ministry, he had to take several steps. He needed to begin by repenting for failing to meet Jenny's needs in a loving, sacrificial, and Christlike way (Ephesians 5:25–30) and for often breaking his promises to her (Ephesians 4:25; Psalm 15:4). Then John's heart motivations needed to be addressed. Was he neglecting his family because he was afraid of failing to measure up to the expectations of the church members? Was he making success in the ministry an idol? Did he falsely believe that the progress of God's work in the church rested solely on his shoulders?

Jenny also needed to seek forgiveness from God and her husband for her sinful outbursts of anger (Matthew 5:21–22) and for confronting John's neglect in an angry and sinful way (Galatians 5:19–21). We encouraged John to treat Jenny in such a way that their marriage would be an example for the church. They began having a short devotion and prayer time together each day. They also agreed to take a walk for half an hour or so before or after dinner so they could share information about what they did during their day. John decided to take Mondays off and to spend at least half of the day enjoying an activity with Jenny, such as an extended hike. John also agreed to turn off his phone during their special times together.

John put additional steps in place to put this plan into action. He spoke with his fellow elders and asked for their help as he sought to renew his marriage. They agreed to be on call during his days off and to help protect his family time. John planned regular time with Jenny (Proverbs 21:5) and put those times on his calendar just like he would a counseling appointment with a church member. When someone asked to meet with him during a time which he had promised to spend with Jenny, he could say, "I am not available then. Can we schedule a different time?" He didn't owe them an explanation that he was going to be enjoying time alone with his wife.

Perhaps the hardest change for John was that he needed to let go of his pastoral perfectionism. Because of his other life responsibilities, he would have to get by with less than twenty hours of study for each sermon, and he would have to skip some committee meetings. I wish

I could say that they immediately followed all our counsel and that their marriage has become a continuous honeymoon. But I can report that they are making progress and that both John and Jenny have hope that their marriage can one day be an example to others.

DOCTOR ROGER AND HIS WIFE VIOLET

Over years of biblical counseling, I have learned that many people in other professions have a similar all-consuming sense of calling which can lead to their neglect of other important priorities, especially their families. Entrepreneurs or small business owners can become workaholics. It is hard to turn down work opportunities, even if one is already overwhelmed. It is hard not to bring work home. When a key client calls with a problem, the business owner will often drop everything to resolve the issue. Similarly, medical doctors typically see their work as a calling. Students also can experience a lifestyle without time boundaries because there is always more that they can do. The same principles of setting priorities, planning, and setting limits on the time and energy we give to our work apply both to employees who are prone to be workaholics and to those whose employers make excessive demands.

Doctor Roger is a renowned specialist who, in addition to doing life-saving surgeries, is engaged in potentially groundbreaking research in his field. His wife Violet is also medically trained but set aside her career to raise their three children. Roger's family enjoyed the economic benefits of his success—a beautiful home, late-model cars, etc. But they didn't see much of Roger. When he was home, he was either too exhausted to engage in family activities or he would go back to his home office and work on his computer. After years of neglect and broken promises, Violet finally insisted that they get biblical counseling.

The advice we offered them was very similar to the advice we offered to Pastor John and his wife Jenny. Roger recognized that he had made an idol of his vocation. He had to stop making excuses and repent, first to God and then to Violet, for his neglect of his family, his failure to honor his wife (1 Peter 3:7), his broken promises, and his pride. "Whoever conceals his transgressions will not prosper, but he who confesses and forsakes them will obtain mercy" (Proverbs 28:13). Violet was challenged to forgive, to set aside bitterness, and to renew hope that their marriage could be revived (Ephesians 4:31–32). Roger embraced the fact that it is God's will that he consistently devotes more time to his family and thus less to his work. He must trust God for the effect this might have on his medical practice and his research. The Lord saw fit to work in a powerful way. Their marriage was transformed. They planned regular time together (Proverbs 21:5). They were even willing to give their testimony, with tears of joy and thankfulness, to one of our biblical counseling classes.

QUESTIONS FOR REFLECTION

1. Did any of the case studies in this chapter help you discern a specific area where you need to implement boundaries or adjust them?

2. Would you have drawn different boundaries in the case studies in this chapter? If so, what biblical basis do you have for the boundaries you would draw? Or are there other biblical wisdom principles or commands that might shed additional light on that specific case?

Chapter 4

APPLYING BIBLICAL PRINCIPLES: A CHILD WHO COMES OUT AS GAY OR TRANSGENDER

Brian and Emily are Christians who sought to raise their four children in a godly way. They regularly had family devotions and went to church. They worked hard as a family, but they also played and laughed. While it grieved them when their daughter Rebecca turned from the faith when she moved out of the house at age eighteen, it was a great shock when, a few years later, Rebecca came out as a lesbian and announced that she was planning to marry her partner the following month. Furthermore, Rebecca said that she would never see or speak with her parents again if they didn't attend the wedding. She even wanted her father to give her away.

Brian and Emily had so many questions. Was her lifestyle choice their fault? Did they fail as parents? What should they do now? What did love for God and love for Rebecca look like in this challenging situation? Many family members, including siblings, aunts, and uncles, had already committed to attend the wedding and had encouraged Brian and Emily to accept that God made Rebecca the way she is. How could this happen in their family? How could they best express their loyal love to God and Rebecca?

While Scripture teaches that parents are responsible to be faithful in raising their children through discipline and instruction (Proverbs 19:18; Ephesians 6:4), the outcome of our parenting is not guaranteed. The book of Proverbs reminds us that the world will also seek to influence our children, who will then, as the Lord noted to Ezekiel, make choices we cannot control (Proverbs 9:13–18; Ezekiel 18:5–18). Jesus also warned that families would be divided according to their response to the gospel (Luke 12:51–53).

The very first family experienced this division, as Abel faithfully worshipped the Lord, but Cain (who was raised by the same parents in the same environment) rejected the voice of God and murdered his brother (Genesis 4:3–8). While Brian and Emily, like the rest of us, were not perfect parents, they are not responsible for the choices Rebecca made. Nor can we say that God made Rebecca this way. Homosexuality is a sinful violation of God's law and God's design (Romans 1:26–27; 1 Corinthians 6:9). Scripture makes it very clear that God can never be blamed for our sin:

> Let no one say when he is tempted, "I am being tempted by God," for God cannot be tempted with evil, and he himself tempts no one. But each person is tempted when he is lured and enticed by his own desire. Then desire when it has conceived gives birth to sin, and sin when it is fully grown brings forth death. (James 1:13–15)

Rebecca had erected a boundary, essentially saying that a condition for entrance into her life was that her parents embrace her lifestyle choice and attend her "wedding." While Brian and Emily should continue to love their daughter and strive to have a relationship with her, they must first seek to please God, which will involve setting limits according to Scripture. Thus, they can't embrace her identity as a lesbian as a good thing. They also agreed that they should not attend Rebecca's celebration. Guests at a wedding are not merely an audience. They are actively involved as witnesses to the making of a marriage covenant, blessing the couple's union and promising to hold the husband and wife responsible for keeping their public vows.

A wedding between two people of the same sex is a counterfeit of God's design, an act of defiance against God, who has defined marriage as a man and a woman making a covenant (Genesis 2:18–25). If Rebecca cuts her parents out of her life because of their unwillingness to attend her wedding, this will be a cost of their loyalty to Christ:

> "Brother will deliver brother over to death, and the father his child, and children will rise against parents and have them put to death, and you will be hated by all for my name's sake. But the one who endures to the end will be saved." (Matthew 10:21–22)

But complete estrangement is not always necessary. I strongly disagree with parents of LGBTQ kids who believe that they must shun their children. Often this shunning is done because of shame or anger over shattered dreams. This shunning often happens when parents make their children into idols. There is nothing in Scripture to justify creating such a boundary. We are called to love even those who treat us as their enemies: "But I say to you who hear, love your enemies, do good to those who hate you, bless those who curse you, pray for those who abuse you" (Luke 6:27–28).

In some cases, an LGBTQ child will still want a relationship with his or her Christian parents. I encouraged Brian and Emily to say something like this: "We love you and are glad that you want a relationship with us, as indicated by inviting us to your event and asking Dad to participate. Since you were raised in our home, you understand what we believe, which explains why we cannot attend. Just as we recognize that you are an adult and that we cannot impose our beliefs on you, we ask you to respect our beliefs." In response to a statement like this one, Rebecca might even back down from her threats to completely cancel her parents. Even though the parents couldn't in good conscience attend the wedding, I believe that they can have a friendly relationship with their daughter and her "friend," including sharing meals. They must always remember that their child's real problem is not her sexuality, but that she is estranged from God. God can save and transform all kinds of sinners (1 Corinthians 6:9–11).

A similar situation arises when a friend or relative comes out as transgender. A son may declare that he is a woman and insist that everyone call him by his new name and refer to him by his chosen pronouns. This problem can be compounded when the parents of a child or teenager are told by school officials that they must support their child's or teenager's chosen gender identity or else the parents could be regarded as abusive, and their child or teenager could be taken out of the home. Again, our response (boundary) is determined by our understanding of God's Word, which states that God made humanity male and female (Genesis 1:27), with each individual being either male or female (Genesis 2:18–23). We cannot lie and deny who God made our children to be, even if we must pay a price in terms of estrangement or other consequences. This may be the area in which Christians in our generation are forced to apply Jesus's warning that we must hate father and mother (Luke 14:26), meaning that they must put Christ above family. This issue also comes up in other spheres. Many are being pressured in workplaces and academic settings to bow the knee to worldly gender ideology with threat of dire consequences. However difficult it may be, we must draw boundaries based on our love for God and our understanding, based on his Word, of what it means to love others: "We must obey God rather than men" (Acts 5:29).

QUESTIONS FOR REFLECTION

1. Did the case study in this chapter help you discern a specific area where you need to implement boundaries or adjust them?

2. Would you have drawn different boundaries in the case study in this chapter? If so, what biblical basis do you have for the boundaries you would draw? Or are there other biblical wisdom principles or commands that might shed additional light on that specific case?

Chapter 5

APPLYING BIBLICAL PRINCIPLES: A SINGLE GIRL WHO HOPES FOR A RING BY SPRING

The desire to marry and have children is honorable and good (Genesis 2:18; Psalm 127:3–5; Proverbs 18:22). But like many good desires, the desire to be married can become idolatrous and ruinous if one puts that desire ahead of his or her commitment to pleasing God.

Tiffany was a college senior whose chief ambition had been to get her "Mrs." degree before graduation. She was a Christian and was involved in both her church and a campus ministry. Tiffany set two primary boundaries from Scripture on her relationships with men. First, she was committed to not having sex until she was married (1 Corinthians 6:18; Hebrews 13:4). The other was that she would only marry a Christian (Deuteronomy 7:3–4; 1 Corinthians 7:39; 2 Corinthians 6:14–18).

But her boundaries were being tested. Because there were not many Christian guys on campus, sometimes when she was asked out by an unbeliever, she agreed on the condition that he also attend the campus ministry with her. None of these relationships worked out. When her mentor warned her about ungodly guys who would pretend to become Christians to date a girl, she decided to no longer date non-Christians.

So, for the past several months, Tiffany had been dating George, whom she met at the campus ministry. They enjoyed spending time together on weekends. Tiffany, however, had some concerns. George didn't seem very interested in spiritual things, other than attending the midweek campus ministry meeting. Another concern was that George would get angry when Tiffany didn't meet his expectations, such as immediately answering every text he sent. He was also often very controlling in other ways. Her greatest concern, however, was that even though they hadn't had sexual intercourse, George kept initiating long periods of heavy kissing and sexual touching. Tiffany felt guilty but told her mentor that she didn't want to hurt George's feelings by telling him to stop. Also, she was afraid of losing him if she didn't meet his expectations. Furthermore, she felt that she had gotten so physically involved with George that another man wouldn't want her because she was dirty. She was also very concerned because even though she kept dropping hints about engagement, George resisted all talk about marriage.

While it is good that Tiffany initially set some limits on her relationships with men, her boundaries weren't tight enough. It isn't enough that a man professes to be a Christian. There are many professing Christian men who are not ready for marriage or perhaps aren't Christians at all. Her mentor encouraged her to read *She's Got the Wrong Guy: Why Smart Women Settle* by Deepak Reju, which warns about men who are controlling, promiscuous, angry, passive, or unwilling to commit. George fits into a few of these categories, which indicates that he probably is "the wrong guy." Tiffany considered breaking up with George, but this would be very hard because she feared that if George didn't marry her, she might never find a husband. The difficulty was compounded by the reality that their physical and emotional intimacy had made Tiffany feel bound to George. Tiffany's main consideration, however, must be to please God (2 Corinthians 5:9).

The root of Tiffany's problem was that she put her desire to be married and to please George above her commitment to loving God and keeping his commandments. Giving in to George's sinful demands wasn't loving him but rather was enabling his sin. Tiffany needed to repent, turning from seeking ultimate fulfillment in the wrong place (Jeremiah 17:5–6) and turning to the Lord as her first love (Jeremiah 17:7-8). She needed to trust that as she walks with him, he will meet her needs, including a husband if that is best. She must patiently wait for a man who loves the Lord with all his heart, a man who will draw her closer to Christ.

Finally, Tiffany agreed that the relationship was leading her into sin and that she must end it. This is an example of the painful, radical amputation described in Matthew 5:29–30. She also learned to trust that if she lost George, God could provide a godly husband in his time. Her mentor encouraged her to remember that if God could provide a husband for Ruth, a Moabite foreigner who had been childless in her first marriage, God could provide a spouse for Tiffany. Her mentor also encouraged

Tiffany to make God the center of her life instead of her desire to get married. For Tiffany this means growing in faith in God's love for her and in the belief that his plans are good. It is scary for her to think that God might not have a spouse for her. But as she prayed and asked for the gift of faith, the Spirit helped her to trust God for each day and to trust that he would provide for her what she needed when she needed it.

Tiffany also needed to reevaluate her limitations on physical intimacy prior to marriage. God has designed the sexual union as a special blessing that expresses the marriage covenant and strengthens the bond between husband and wife (Genesis 2:24; Hebrews 13:4). The physical intimacy which is reserved for marriage is not limited to the act of sexual intercourse. God has designed other sexual touching as a way of uniting a couple and preparing them for full sexual union. Sexual touching between two people who are not married to each other can create a bond that can be hard to break (1 Corinthians 6:16).

Further, Tiffany needed to realize that physical touching may mean different things to a man and a woman. What a woman may take as an expression of affection and devotion might be experienced by a man as sexual arousal regardless of commitment. Our bodies and sexuality belong to our spouses (1 Corinthians 7:3–4). If one is not yet married, that person's body belongs to their future spouse. That person should not give away prior to marriage that which will belong to that person's spouse after marriage. When I was single, a friend offered a wise "boundary" for dating. He said, "Treat the woman you are dating like you hope the guy who is out tonight with your future wife is treating her. Don't do anything you or she would regret in the future.

One day you will wish that you had only kissed your wife." Tiffany could be comforted in God's forgiveness for past sin while committing to wait for a man who would "flee youthful passions and pursue righteousness, faith, love, and peace, along with those who call on the Lord from a pure heart" (2 Timothy 2:22).

QUESTIONS FOR REFLECTION

1. Did the case study in this chapter help you discern a specific area where you need to implement boundaries or adjust them?

2. Would you have drawn different boundaries in the case study in this chapter? If so, what biblical basis do you have for the boundaries you would draw? Or are there other biblical wisdom principles or commands that might shed additional light on that specific case?

Chapter 6

APPLYING BIBLICAL PRINCIPLES: IN-LAWS WHO ACT LIKE OUTLAWS

Mike and Liz are happily married. Mike is a project manager for a construction company, Liz is a teacher, and they have two elementary-aged children. Mike and Liz get along well with each other and are on the same page about most things, but they have one significant problem. Liz feels that Mike's mother, Patty, doesn't treat her with respect. Liz says that when Mike's parents come to visit, her mother-in-law subtly criticizes Liz's housekeeping, cooking, and parenting. Liz also complains that Patty is controlling and takes over when she visits, adding that Patty deliberately excludes Liz from participation in family activities Patty organizes.

Mike doesn't notice these slights, and when Liz complains to him, he tells her that she should just turn the other cheek (Matthew 5:39). Liz is not satisfied with this response, so the tension between her and Mike is growing. They finally agree to seek biblical counseling. Their counselor quickly realizes that Mike tends to be nonconfrontational and that his approach (like that of his father) to his mother's domineering tendency has been submissive silence or appeasement. Liz, however, is not a conflict avoider, and she finds it very difficult to overlook Patty's unkind words and actions toward her.

Their counselor encouraged them to make pleasing God their primary motivation when seeking a solution to their problem (2 Corinthians 5:9). They also should strive to understand and love one another through this challenging situation (Philippians 2:1–5). When wronged, Liz can still, with the Lord's help, not give in to anger and can demonstrate the fruit of the Spirit, including patience and self-control (Galatians 5:22–23). She can strive to maintain an attitude of forgiveness: "Above all, keep loving one another earnestly, since love covers a multitude of sins" (1 Peter 4:8). It pleases God for her to overlook some of the unkind things Patty says (Proverbs 19:11) and strive to love her in a Christlike way.

But Mike should also recognize that the Lord wants his relationship with his wife to have priority even over his relationship with his parents (Genesis 2:24). He should strive to understand how Patty's unkindness affects Liz, and he should take her concerns seriously: "Likewise, husbands, live with your wives in an understanding way" (1 Peter 3:7a). Furthermore, there are limits (boundaries) to the amount of mistreatment he should expect Liz to endure. There are times when his duty to God and his wife will be to intervene. He must be prepared to overcome his tendency to appease his mother (fear of man—Proverbs 29:25) and confront her most egregious mistreatment of Liz gently but firmly (Galatians 6:1).

While the counselor couldn't tell Mike and Liz the exact point at which overlooking ends and confronting becomes necessary, he encouraged them to discuss this point ahead of Patty's visits and to pray together for wisdom. In addition, he encouraged Mike to make time to communicate privately with Liz when they are around his parents and to listen sympathetically to her concerns. Their counselor reminded Mike that it wasn't loving to his mother to let her continue to treat Liz unkindly, nor was it loving to his children to let them watch while his mother was unkind to Liz.

Sometime later, when his parents were visiting, Mike found it necessary to gently confront his mother when he heard Patty unfairly criticizing Liz. Even though Patty didn't respond as well as Mike hoped, Liz was greatly encouraged that he was willing to stand up for her. Mike and Liz also talked about whether, at some point, they might have to limit Patty's visits if she is unwilling to treat Liz with respect. Mike was learning that love says no to sins and learning to support his wife by having her back when Patty picked on her. Because Liz could see Mike's love for her in his response, her respect for him grew, as did her tolerance for slights by her mother-in-law.

VALID REASONS FOR CREATING DISTANCE IN RELATIONSHIPS

You can see that how Mike and Liz dealt with Patty had a lot of gray areas involved. When that happens, you must take your time and seek wisdom to know how to love God and love others in a challenging relationship. At other times, it's clear that there needs to be some distance in a family relationship.

For example, Christine is happily married to Franz. They have been married for fifteen years and have four children. Early on in their marriage, when they would visit her parents, Christine's father would often express out-of-control anger (Proverbs 25:28), especially after he had consumed too much alcohol. On one occasion Franz drove his family for over four hours to see Christine's parents. Not long after they arrived, Christine's father became verbally abusive to one of their children after he accidentally spilled his drink. Franz tried to calm the situation (Matthew 5:9; Romans 12:18), but his father-in-law became more belligerent and threatening.

Franz decided that his only option, considering his God-given responsibility to protect his wife and children, was to put his family back in the car and to return home. Franz and Christine do not intend to be permanently estranged from her parents (by canceling them). They continue to talk with them over the phone and to send them gifts and cards. They are willing to try again to spend time with her parents, but they made it clear (in a sense, setting a boundary) that if the previous incident was repeated, then they would again have to leave.

There can be valid reasons for creating distance in relationships. Franz and Christine were right to leave her parents' home when her father became verbally abusive to their family. The overarching principle of making it your aim to love God and love people means that we protect others from anger and hate, as well as verbal, physical, and sexual abuse. Separating yourselves and others from those relationships is a way to love both the abused and the abuser. Love says no to the abuser's sin. Children who have been victims of sexual or physical abuse have the right to be safe. Women who are abused by their husbands should be protected. God is firmly on the side of the vulnerable.

There is, however, often a failure to distinguish between heinous acts of oppression and the ordinary shortcomings of loving parents. Abigail Shrier, in her book *Bad Therapy: Why the Kids Aren't Growing Up*, suggests that in many cases ostracized parents have not been abusive but that the main cause of estrangement is that young adults have been told (often by therapists) to blame their parents for all their troubles. Shrier also points out the harm which such family estrangement brings upon multiple generations.

Sadly, some adult children have canceled their parents because they were disciplined (nonabusively) when they were young, restricted from certain worldly influences, and forced to attend church and family devotions. Many Christian mothers and fathers have faced the heartbreak of children who have come out as homosexual or transgender and who insist that all family members embrace their new identity, attend their weddings, and use their pronouns, threatening complete estrangement of those who won't comply.[1]

Of course, there are no perfect parents. We will all look back with regret upon our parenting failures. Scripture reminds us that all earthly parents will fall short of God's perfect fatherly discipline because all parents are sinners (Romans 3:23). While we are responsible for being faithful parents (Ephesians 6:4), our children, as they become adults, will make decisions for which they are responsible. They can't blame us for their choices, nor should we blame ourselves. I have written more extensively elsewhere regarding why children turn out the way that they do.[2]

When family members choose to cancel each other, those who grieve over the estrangement can and should seek to make peace (Romans 12:18), but it is not always in their power to do so.

QUESTIONS FOR REFLECTION

1. Did the case studies in this chapter help you discern a specific area where you need to implement boundaries or adjust them?

2. Would you have drawn different boundaries? If so, what biblical basis do you have for the boundaries you would draw? Or are there other biblical wisdom principles or commands that might shed additional light on that specific case?

Chapter 7

APPLYING BIBLICAL PRINCIPLES: SEXUAL BOUNDARIES IN MARRIAGE

Marriage begins with a covenant in which both parties draw a line of protection around their relationship. Both husband and wife agree that they will stay within sexual boundaries both positively, by being devoted to one another sexually, and negatively, by not having sexual contact with others (who are out of bounds).

SETTING BOUNDARIES AFTER AN AFFAIR

We counseled a couple where the wife, Karen, had been unfaithful to her husband, Ronald. He had forgiven her but wanted them to establish some safeguards for their marriage, including mutual accountability. She, however, insisted that he had no right to know about her interactions with other men (including shared texts and meals), claiming that insisting on this level of transparency would be too controlling. She said that Ronald must trust her. While there are many issues in this situation, the fundamental issue was that Karen needed to be reminded that when she married Ronald, she agreed, before God and witnesses, to be limited by the boundaries of their covenant. She also needed to be warned against proud self-confidence. Scripture provides us with such warnings because we are all sinful and vulnerable (1 Corinthians 10:12). So, it is wise to set boundaries for the purpose of protecting their commitment before God and their love for one another.

Although we didn't recommend that Ronald act as a detective, trying to control Karen's every move, we did recommend that she respond positively to his request to be updated on her ongoing interactions with other men. This was a concrete way that Karen could demonstrate to Ronald her renewed commitment to her marriage vows and, thus, a way to love him. Ronald can show his love to Karen by not constantly bringing up her infidelity and not trying to micromanage her life. Some couples agree to follow what is known as the Billy Graham Rule, in which spouses agree not to engage in intimate conversations nor to spend time alone in potentially compromising situations with someone of the opposite sex.

BOUNDARIES APPLIED TO MARITAL INTIMACY

Many couples experience conflicts over sex. It is rare that a husband and wife will have perfectly matched libidos (or sleep schedules). We have counseled couples in which one would like sex virtually every day, while once a week (or month) is plenty for the other. Some couples are no longer physically intimate. In such cases, it is important to determine why. Couples go through different seasons, with different levels of sexual interest, in their marriages—newlyweds, young parents, middle-aged individuals, etc. Marital conflict often occurs because of different expectations. A husband may remind his wife of Scripture, which encourages him to resist temptation by finding sexual delight with his wife:

> Drink water from your own cistern, flowing water from your own well. . . . Let your fountain be blessed, and rejoice in the wife of your youth, a lovely deer, a graceful doe. Let her breasts fill you at all times with delight; be intoxicated always in her love. (Proverbs 5:15, 18–19)

Meanwhile, his wife may be so exhausted by their small children at the end of the day that sex is the last thing on her mind. All she wants is sleep. A conflict may be brewing. Both may be tempted to be selfish. How can such conflicts be resolved?

Paul offers wisdom about how the Lord wants husbands and wives to care for each other sexually:

> The husband should give to his wife her conjugal rights, and likewise the wife to her husband. For the wife does not have authority over her own body, but the husband does. Likewise the husband does not have authority over his own body, but the wife does. Do not deprive one another, except perhaps by agreement for a limited time, that you may devote yourselves to prayer; but then come together again, so that Satan may not tempt you because of your lack of self-control. (1 Corinthians 7:3–5)

Selfish, abusive husbands have misused this text to demand sex whenever, wherever, and however they require it. A husband who loves his wife in a sacrificial, Christlike way (Ephesians 5:25–30) would never try to force his spouse to have sex with him against her will. He should be considerate of her needs and desires. Every husband must respect his wife's freedom to say no.

A related issue is that some husbands try to get their wives to participate in sex acts which the wife finds to be painful or demeaning. We had a case in which a young wife called us late at night crying because her husband was asking her to participate in a certain sexual practice which she found to be unpleasant. Often these demands are fueled by the husband's indulgence in pornography, which promotes the vile lie (among other lies) that the ultimate sexual experience occurs when men selfishly indulge their lust through sex acts that demean women. A husband who is indulging in pornography or whose views of sex have been corrupted by porn probably needs some godly counseling/mentoring. He must repent of his sin, and he needs to relearn sex as God designed it.[1] A wife has the right to say no to any sexual request that violates her conscience, and a loving husband would never pressure his wife to go against her conscience. "For whatever does not proceed from faith is sin" (Romans 14:23).

While we abhor the misuse of Paul's teaching in 1 Corinthians 7, this passage does offer wisdom for many of the ordinary sexual difficulties husbands and wives experience. Some have wrongly taught that a wife should never have sex with her husband unless she is eager to do so. While it is wrong for one spouse to compel the other to have sex, we should remember that our sexuality has been given to us by God for the benefit of our spouses and that we have conjugal duties to each other (1 Corinthians 7:3–5). We are to consider the interests and needs of others and not just our own desires (Philippians 2:3–4).

Tim and Kathy Keller put it well: "Each partner in marriage is to be most concerned not with getting sexual pleasure but *giving* it. In short, the greatest sexual pleasure should be the pleasure of seeing your spouse getting pleasure."[2] Kathy writes about how they overcame some of their struggles:

> When we stopped trying to perform and just started trying to simply love one another in sex, things started to move ahead. We stopped worrying about our performance. And we stopped worrying about what we were getting and started to say, "Well, what can we do just to give something to the other?"[3]

In practical terms, this may mean that the spouse with the stronger interest in sex considers his spouse's desires, including her need for rest. He can find joy and pleasure by sometimes sacrificially setting aside his desires and putting her needs first. On the other hand, his spouse, who has less sexual desire, doesn't merely consider her own needs but wants her husband to feel loved and fulfilled. A spouse who is tired might promise intimacy at a specified time in the near future. The biblical standard is that spouses do not establish a boundary of selfishness as they strive to bless one another.

Sexual intimacy in some marriages has been impacted by trauma over past abuse, guilt over past sin, or unscriptural teaching that sex is somehow unclean. Godly counsel may help a couple to overcome the effects of these harmful influences. This will require patience on the part of both husband and wife. They should keep in mind God's good purposes for sex in marriage, which binds a husband and wife together as an expression of the marriage covenant (Genesis 2:24). Out of the love that husbands and wives have for one another, God gives them children (Genesis 1:28; Psalm 127:3–5). Again, the Kellers put it well:

> Indeed, sex is perhaps the most powerful God-created way to help you give your entire self to another human being. Sex is God's appointed way for two people to say to one another, "I belong completely, permanently, and exclusively to you."[4]

QUESTIONS FOR REFLECTION

1. Did the case studies in this chapter help you discern a specific area where you need to implement boundaries or adjust them?

2. Would you have drawn different boundaries? If so, what biblical basis do you have for the boundaries you would draw? Or are there other biblical wisdom principles or commands that might shed additional light on that specific case?

Chapter 8

APPLYING BIBLICAL PRINCIPLES: DEALING WITH PAST ABUSE

Joan had a difficult childhood. She grew up in a home in which her parents often disciplined her in anger, sometimes causing welts and bruises. But worst of all, her older brother would come into her room at night and sexually molest her. She once tried to tell her mother, but her mother did nothing to keep Joan safe. When Joan went away to college, a friend shared the gospel with her. Joan became a Christian, was baptized, joined a church, and experienced tremendous spiritual growth.

When Joan was in her late twenties, she married a godly man, Bob, who aspired to be a pastor. They had four children together and served as a family in a local church, where Bob was a vocational minister. In the early years of their marriage, they had little contact with Joan's family. Then Joan and her husband decided to try to reconnect with them. They decided to meet with her parents and her brother (who was now married, with a family of his own) to share their faith and to offer forgiveness for the abuse

Applying Biblical Principles: Dealing with Past Abuse 61

that happened when she was a girl. While her family was glad to see her, along with her children and her husband, they claimed not to remember the sexual abuse and didn't apologize.

Joan and her husband Bob met with a biblical counselor to seek advice about what they should do. Joan was able to talk through her past abuse and to see it from a biblical perspective. She had been terribly wronged and was not responsible for the evil done against her. While she was sad that she could not be fully reconciled with her family members because they had not repented, she had an attitude of grace and forgiveness.

She was thankful for how God had saved her and led her into a happy marriage with wonderful children, and she was thankful for a life of fruitful ministry. Joan determined that she was not required to report her brother's acts from many years ago, so she decided not to make it a legal matter.[1] She wanted to honor the Lord by keeping the fifth commandment—the commandment to honor her parents—but she still had to decide what boundaries to place upon her relationship with her parents and her brother.

The counselor told Joan and Bob that he could not tell them from Scripture exactly which limits to impose. Some victims in Joan's position might choose to have no personal contact with their family members because being with them would be too disturbing. Joan was free to choose this option. In such a case, she could maintain some limited contact with her family (e.g., cards or calls) for the sake of gospel witness and with the hope that reconciliation could take place in the future. Another option would have been to see her parents from time to time, but not with her brother present. Joan instead made the choice to spend time with her entire family on special occasions. She and Bob determined, however, that they would not bring their children with them on the occasions when her brother would be present.

QUESTIONS FOR REFLECTION

1. Did the case study in this chapter help you discern a specific area where you need to implement boundaries or adjust them?

2. Would you have drawn different boundaries? If so, what biblical basis do you have for the boundaries you would draw? Or are there other biblical wisdom principles or commands that might shed additional light on that specific case?

Chapter 9

APPLYING BIBLICAL PRINCIPLES: FINANCIAL BOUNDARIES

Drawing financial boundaries with family and friends can be challenging. On the one hand, Scripture calls us to be generous toward those in need: "Whoever is generous to the poor lends to the Lord, and he will repay him for his deed" (Proverbs 19:17). We are also called to be good stewards who take care of the needs of our families (1 Timothy 5:8). On the other hand, we are told not to give to those who are lazy and refuse to work (2 Thessalonians 3:10). If you have a friend or family member who is continually asking for money from you, then examine your heart and seek out wise counselors who can help you discern what actions will best show love for God and others in the particulars of your situation. I have written a book containing a more detailed look at wise financial boundaries.[1]

SETTING FINANCIAL BOUNDARIES WITH PARENTS

Lenora, aged twenty-five, is a nurse who lives with her parents in their rented house. She helps around the house and contributes to expenses. Lenora has been dating Kenny for a year, and she expects that they will be engaged soon. Lenora's parents, Ed and Lucy, have never been good with money. They often overspend, and they have significant credit card debt. Recently Ed and Lucy decided to replace their ten-year-old car with a new vehicle. But no bank or dealer would lend them the money, so they asked Lenora to cosign their loan. What should Lenora do? She believes that God wants her to honor her parents and to be generous. But she also knows that she should be a good steward. The pressure upon her is compounded by the fact that her family's culture expects those who can help to help in this way, especially because she has a good income.

From a biblical perspective, what is a loving response to this situation? Loving and honoring her parents does not mean that she must always do what they ask. While Lenora is free to choose to cosign (or to give them money), she also is free to say no. There are many scriptural reasons why it would probably be unwise for her to agree to her parents' request. First, Scripture warns that making oneself liable for the debts of others is risky and ordinarily foolish. Proverbs 22:26–27 gives a vivid warning: "Be not one of those who give pledges, who put up security for debts. If you have nothing with which to pay, why should your bed be taken from under you?" (see also Proverbs 6:1–5). If the bank believed that her parents could pay for the car, they would not have required a cosigner. One day Lenora could be held liable for the entire debt. By coming to their rescue, Lenora may be enabling her parents' ongoing financial irresponsibility, which would ultimately be unloving and would likely result in her being asked to bail them out again in the future. Furthermore, Lenora may soon "leave father and mother" and establish her own family with her new husband (Genesis 2:24). My church had a case similar to Lenora's, in which a new couple had difficulty securing a loan for their new house because the wife's credit was tied up with that of her parents.

SETTING FINANCIAL BOUNDARIES WITH FRIENDS

Robin's group of female friends from college were planning to go on a cruise during spring break, which would also serve as a bachelorette party for Elaine, who would be getting married shortly after graduation. Most of the other girls were from wealthy families and would have no trouble getting their parents to pay for the trip. Robin came from a working-class family that barely makes ends meet. She could have asked her parents to help, but they had already made sacrifices for her to complete her education. She also suspected that they would have to borrow to come up with the money.

Robin considered using her own credit card to pay for the trip but realized that this would put her near her credit limit. And because she had student debt and didn't yet have a job lined up after graduation, she didn't know how she would pay off the debt. Robin had always been a bit ashamed by the fact that she couldn't keep up with the other girls, who had plenty of money to spend on clothes and entertainment. It would be embarrassing to tell them that she couldn't go. They would be disappointed in her. Perhaps they would reject her as the poor girl who just didn't fit in. She wondered if she could make up some excuse—like a sick grandmother who needed her that week.

First, Robin had to examine her heart. Did she covet what the other girls had (Colossians 3:5)? Was she being controlled by the fear of man (Proverbs 29:25)? Was her concern that her friends would judge and reject her a judgmental failure to assume the best of them, for "Love . . . hopes all things" (1 Corinthians 13:7)? Was she guilty of discontentment instead of being thankful for the many ways in which God had richly blessed her (Philippians 4:11–12; 1 Timothy 6:8)? Lying to her friends by making up a story about a sick grandmother was not an option (Ephesians 4:25). Robin also needed to consider the danger of debt, which can put one into bondage: "The borrower is the slave of the lender" (Proverbs 22:7). She couldn't afford to take on thousands of dollars of additional borrowing. Ultimately, she realized that she must tell her friends no, even if they reject her or look down on her for not being able to afford the trip, and be content with what God has provided and will provide for her (Philippians 4:11–13).

SETTING FINANCIAL BOUNDARIES WITH THOSE ASKING FOR A HANDOUT

While serving at a local church, we often had people coming to our building asking for a handout. Sometimes we would offer them some of the food we kept on hand. There was one man, Tony, who was especially persistent, even quoting Scripture as he tried to persuade us to give him money: "Give to the one who begs from you, and do not refuse the one who would borrow from you" (Matthew 5:42). Tony also was prepared to discuss and debate other matters of theology and Bible interpretation.

Tony claimed to be a Christian, so I asked him if I could contact his church to see if they would want to help him or at least to give us a good report about him. He said that he was not a member of any church. I asked if I could contact his family to see if they would want to come to his rescue. I was able to reach his brother, who said that the family had tried in various ways to help Tony find employment or gain stability in his life, but that Tony refused any help which would force him to give up any of the control he had over his life. I realized that I was in a situation that Paul had warned the church in Thessalonica about: "Now we command you, brothers, in the name of our Lord Jesus Christ, that you keep away from any brother who is walking in idleness and not in accord with the tradition that you received from us" (2 Thessalonians 3:6). I determined that it would neither please God nor help Tony for me to give him what he demanded. When Tony realized that I wasn't going to budge, he finally went on his way.

SETTING FINANCIAL BOUNDARIES WITH AN INHERITANCE

Stella and her husband Marcus had been married eighteen years and had four children. Stella was committed to her marriage and wanted to be a godly, submissive wife. Marcus was a skilled laborer and could bring in a good income, but he was bad at managing money. Whenever they would get ahead financially, rather than saving for the future, Marcus would take time off until he needed to work again to pay the bills.

Stella's mother had recently passed away and left Stella an inheritance of over two hundred thousand dollars. Stella wanted to invest her mother's money so that it could help provide for their retirement and their children's education. Marcus's view was that the money belonged to both equally, and that, since he was the husband, Stella must follow his leadership in how the money was to be spent. Marcus was talking about purchasing a new top-of-the-line fishing boat and taking several months off to enjoy it. He wanted to invest the rest in starting a new business he had read about online.

Stella worried that her inheritance could be completely squandered within a few years and wondered if she had any right to maintain control over it. To address her concerns, Stella suggested that they seek counsel together from their pastor. The pastor reminded Marcus that the Lord had not given husbands leadership in the home so that they could act selfishly. Rather, husbands are to use their authority to serve their wives selflessly and sacrificially, as a more specific application of how all Christians are to treat each other (Ephesians 5:25–30; John 13:1–15). He admonished Marcus to follow Solomon's exhortation to imitate the ant by working hard and preparing for the future (Proverbs 6:6–8). He also warned Marcus of the deceptive peril of laziness: "A little sleep, a little slumber, a little folding of the hands to rest, and poverty will come upon you like a robber, and want like an armed man" (Proverbs 6:10–11). He also encouraged Marcus to trust his wife's greater wisdom in financial matters, an area in which she reflected the biblical ideal for wives (Proverbs 31:11–12, 26).

Sadly, Marcus didn't appreciate the pastor's counsel. He walked out of the session saying, "I am the head of the house, and my wife must submit to me. I expect her to turn over the money as soon as she receives it." In the next session, the pastor and his wife met alone with Stella. They considered the story of Abigail in 1 Samuel 25. When her husband Nabal's folly threatened the safety and security of their family, Abigail took decisive action and, against her husband's express wishes, used family resources to avert disaster (1 Samuel 25:10–20). There are other cases in Scripture in which married women maintained some control over financial resources (Luke 8:3; Proverbs 31:10ff). In this case, it would not be loving Marcus to allow him to oversee a considerable sum of money. The pastor advised Stella that she was free to maintain control over her inheritance and to use or invest it as she believed to be best for her family. The pastor and his wife offered to support her as she conveyed her decision to Marcus.

QUESTIONS FOR REFLECTION

1. Did the case studies in this chapter help you discern a specific area where you need to implement boundaries or adjust them?

2. Would you have drawn different boundaries? If so, what biblical basis do you have for the boundaries you would draw? Or are there other biblical wisdom principles or commands that might shed additional light on that specific case?

Chapter 10

APPLYING BIBLICAL PRINCIPLES: FAILURE TO LAUNCH

Ron was twenty-nine and still living with his parents, Linda and Mark. Ron graduated from college with a general business degree four years ago, but he hadn't been able to maintain stable employment. When he did get a job, Ron would soon become bored and either quit or be fired for failure to show up for work. Linda and Mark lived in a spacious home, so there was plenty of room for Ron. They were also well-off, so it wasn't a strain on their finances for them to provide Ron with a car and to pay most of his bills. Sometimes when Ron stayed up all night drinking and playing video games with his friends, Mark would become angry and want to kick him out of the house. But Linda was reluctant to put much pressure on Ron because he had always been a sensitive child, and he now claimed that he couldn't work because he was suffering from depression. Ron also believed that his inability to keep a job was related to his having inherited the disease of alcoholism. How and where to set boundaries with Ron had become a significant point of tension between Mark and Linda, who finally sought biblical counsel.

First, their counselor asked what their primary goal was with Ron. Linda wanted Ron to be safe and happy. Mark wanted Ron to get a job and get out of the house. Their counselor sought to reorient their goal to be that they honor and please God as they navigate this trial (2 Corinthians 5:9). They each would have to do some hard things. Their counselor encouraged them to pray together daily asking God to make them wise (James 1:5), to keep them united, and to help them to walk in the Spirit throughout this process.

He also explained that Scripture contains the wisdom they need, and that God's Word speaks specifically to difficult situations with adult children (Deuteronomy 21:18–21; 1 Samuel 2:22–29; 1 Kings 1:6). Both parents must honor and love God above their son (1 Samuel 2:29). Excusing and enabling Ron's sin will bring misery to everyone (Proverbs 29:15). Those who are foolish usually need consequences to get them to change (Proverbs 26:3). To enable Ron to continue in his sin would not be loving in the long run.

The counselor further suggested that they require that Ron meet with a godly counselor to investigate his depression and possible addiction to alcohol. For Ron to be allowed to remain in the home, he must meet regularly with the counselor, follow the counselor's recommendations, and allow the counselor to speak with Mark and Linda regarding Ron's progress. Assuming that there is no medical reason why Ron couldn't hold down a job, Linda and Mark agreed to require that Ron either work or seek employment for a minimum of forty hours a week.

In addition, Ron would be required to do his share of the work around the house and to pay nominal rent (which his parents planned to keep and return to him when he moves out). If Ron was willing to follow these guidelines, he and his parents would evaluate every six months whether it would be best for him to remain or to move out. If Ron was unwilling to meet these conditions, he would be required to move out immediately.

QUESTIONS FOR REFLECTION

1. Did the case study in this chapter help you discern a specific area where you need to implement boundaries or adjust them?

2. Would you have drawn different boundaries? If so, what biblical basis do you have for the boundaries you would draw? Or are there other biblical wisdom principles or commands that might shed additional light on that specific case?

Chapter 11

APPLYING BIBLICAL PRINCIPLES: ADDICTED TO SCREENS

Emma, who had always been a cheerful, compliant child, had been begging her parents, Sam and Becky, for a smartphone since she was nine, which was the age at which most of her friends had one. Finally, on her thirteenth birthday, they gave in. At first, Emma was very happy, but over time, Sam and Becky noticed that Emma had become moody and had distanced herself from her family. Her grades dropped. When they purchased the smartphone, Sam and Becky tried to limit the apps to which Emma had access and the amount of time she could spend on screens each day. They now realize that as the months passed, they didn't monitor Emma's activity as closely as they had at the beginning. Their daughter had been spending several hours a day on her phone, including sneaking it into her bedroom at night. She had found a way to install the forbidden social media apps and had become a major user.

It has been estimated that teens, on average, spend more than eight hours a day on screens for entertainment,[1] which doesn't include school and work screen time. This represents a massive increase since smartphones were first introduced. Even when they aren't fully engaged with their smartphones, teens may be distracted by as many as two hundred notifications per day.[2] Jonathan Haidt cites evidence suggesting that the proliferation of smartphones has led to radical increases in depression and anxiety among teenagers, especially girls, who are vulnerable to hurtful comparisons and cruel words on social media. Boys are more vulnerable to pornography and video game addiction. In both cases, parents need to set and enforce limits.[3] Cloud and Townsend[4], along with Haidt,[5] offer some useful practical suggestions for parents. God calls us as parents to discipline our children (Ephesians 6:4), which essentially means that we must establish and enforce boundaries. Our children need our help so that they will please God (2 Corinthians 5:9) by being wise and diligent in the use of their time (Proverbs 10:5). Sam and Becky decided to put Emma on a one-month smartphone fast, after which they limited her use of the phone to one hour a day and in the presence of parents. When Emma was not using her phone, her parents would have it. The hope is that as Sam and Becky also offer wise instruction in addition to setting these rules, Emma will grow up to set her own wise boundaries which honor God.

QUESTIONS FOR REFLECTION

1. Did the case study in this chapter help you discern a specific area where you need to implement boundaries or adjust them?

2. Would you have drawn different boundaries? If so, what biblical basis do you have for the boundaries you would draw? Or are there other biblical wisdom principles or commands that might shed additional light on that specific case?

CONCLUSION

The problems that occur in life and in our relationships are complicated. But applying the overall principles of love for God and love for others can give concrete, practical direction in even the most tangled situation. Hopefully the case studies included here have helped you see how making your goal to please God through loving him and loving others can give you solid direction in how to respond in confusing situations.

Often you may feel overwhelmed and confused by the pressures other people put on you. But you can always find direction and help when you keep this question at the forefront of your mind: *How, according to my understanding of God's Word, can I best please God and love others well in this situation?* You can prayerfully ask God for wisdom (James 1:5) and act in faith and hope. And when you notice that you aren't loving God and people with your words and actions, you can ask God to forgive you because of Jesus's death on the cross for you and ask others for forgiveness as well. Being a Christian means that we can get a whole new start to each day as we rely on God's mercy to us.

Conclusion

Remember, also, that being busy is not a bad thing! God wants us to be productive, as indicated by how he put a prayer for productivity in Scripture (Psalm 90:17). He saved us by grace for good works (Ephesians 2:10). But because we are finite and the demands upon us are many, we can't say yes to everyone. We must be good stewards of our time. If our focus is people pleasing, people may take advantage of us, causing us to feel overwhelmed and miserable. Even worse, we are neglecting God's call upon our lives when we rush to fulfill every demand that people make of us. But the alternative to pleasing people is not selfishness. Rather, our lives are to be governed by our commitment to pleasing God and loving others according to our understanding of his priorities for our lives. Even though what is best may not be clear in every situation, we seek wisdom through the Word of God and prayer. We walk in the steps of Jesus, who did not capitulate to the demands of men, nor did he please himself (Romans 15:3). Instead, he devoted himself to pleasing his Father (John 8:29). You can ask for the Spirit to help you, every day, discern what is good and pleasing to God and then to step into those good works. There is much peace to have as we live for pleasing God instead of pleasing people.

Consider making Paul's prayer for the Colossians your daily prayer and see how the Spirit will help and guide you:

> And so, from the day we heard, we have not ceased to pray for you, asking that you may be filled with the knowledge of his will in all spiritual wisdom and understanding, so as to walk in a manner worthy of the Lord, fully pleasing to him:

bearing fruit in every good work and increasing in the knowledge of God; being strengthened with all power, according to his glorious might, for all endurance and patience with joy; giving thanks to the Father, who has qualified you to share in the inheritance of the saints in light. He has delivered us from the domain of darkness and transferred us to the kingdom of his beloved Son, in whom we have redemption, the forgiveness of sins. (Colossians 1:9–14)

Appendix

A BIBLICAL PERSPECTIVE ON CLOUD AND TOWNSEND'S TREATMENT OF BOUNDARIES

Because the approach to setting boundaries which I advocate in this book is different from that advocated by Cloud and Townsend I offer this brief critique of their writing.

POSITIVE FEATURES OF THE *BOUNDARIES* BOOK

There are several aspects of the *Boundaries* book we can appreciate. The authors are openly Christian, and the book affirms the Christian faith. They use an immense amount of Scripture. They deserve credit for vividly describing a significant, widespread problem. They sincerely want to help people, and they are right that we all need to set limits on relationships. Their book is well organized and easy to read. They portray realistic, practical examples of the problems caused by the failure to set limits on relationships. They offer some helpful, practical advice. I especially appreciate their biblical (and countercultural) emphasis that children need limits and that children must be disciplined. They offer wise warnings against unregulated social media for teens. They encourage parents to allow their children (even adult children) to take responsibility for the consequences of those children's choices.[1] I also appreciate that they encourage those whose boundaries have been violated to be willing to graciously offer forgiveness.[2]

SIGNIFICANT CONCERNS

While there are many things to appreciate about this book, we would do well to examine some points of concern regarding the authors' approach to boundaries and how these shortcomings could negatively impact readers' understanding of Scripture, the nature of their relationship with God, and how to express anger.

Scripture is often misused

While I am glad that Cloud and Townsend acknowledge the wisdom and authority of God's Word, the way they use Scripture to support their teaching frequently has little or nothing to do with the meaning and purpose of the text in its biblical context. As Ed Welch points out, "The Boundary series contains biblical references throughout as a means to illustrate Scripture's emphasis on boundaries, but psychological theory seems to be the basic reason that this metaphor receives attention."[3] For example, the authors apply Jesus's warning not to store up treasure on earth (Matthew 6:19–21) to say that boundaries "guard our treasures."[4] This passage has nothing to do with protecting ourselves from people who violate our limits, but rather Jesus is calling us to devote ourselves to God's kingdom and not waste our lives pursuing earthly treasures, which will one day be destroyed.

My greatest concern about their use of the Bible is that texts are often taken out of their redemptive context, thus providing practical, moralistic self-help advice apart from the centrality of the gospel. For example, we are told that Philippians 2:12–13 teaches that "We are also commanded to play an active role in seeking our desires."[5] This passage is not about seeking our own desires, but rather about how we are called to pursue God's good purpose in our lives:

> Therefore, my beloved, as you have always obeyed, so now, not only as in my presence but much more in my absence, work out your own salvation with fear and trembling, for it is God who works in you, both to will and to work for his good pleasure. (Philippians 2:12–13)

Another example is their use of John 16:33, where Jesus warns that we will have trouble in the world, to say that we will have trouble when we try to maintain our boundaries.[6] The trouble we will have in the world is the result of our commitment to Christ, not because of our efforts to guard our personal boundaries. Proverbs 4:23, "Keep your heart with all vigilance, for from it flow the springs of life," is referenced several times to support their approach to setting personal boundaries: "When we watch over our hearts (the home of our treasures) we guard them."[7] This passage has nothing to do with protecting ourselves from the intrusions of others. Rather, the point of this proverb is that we must guard our hearts from sin and that we must pursue wisdom in the fear of the Lord.

Yet another example is how 1 John 4:19, "We love because he first loved us," is improperly explained: "We learn to be loving because we are loved. . . . We can't love when we aren't loved. . . . We can't value or treasure our souls when they haven't been valued or treasured" (by other people).[8] This Bible passage is not speaking of our being enabled to love because others love and treasure us, but rather of our being enabled to love because we have first experienced God's gracious love to us. The reflection of redemptive love enables us to show love to people who don't value and treasure us.

Some assertions contradict sound biblical doctrine

One chapter is entitled, "Boundaries and God."[9] They write, "He (God) respects our no. He tries neither to control nor nag us. . . . He respects boundaries."[10] At best, these statements could easily be misunderstood or misleading. Scripture tells us that we were once "dead in [our] trespasses and sins" (Ephesians 2:1), enemies of God (Romans 5:10), who actively suppressed the knowledge of God as it was revealed to us in creation and conscience (Romans 1:18–32; 2:14–15). We wanted to be autonomous and to have nothing to do with God, but he chose to intrude by bringing us from death to life:

> But God, being rich in mercy, because of the great love with which he loved us, even when we were dead in our trespasses, made us alive together with Christ—by grace you have been saved—and raised us up with him and seated us with him in the heavenly places in Christ Jesus. (Ephesians 2:4–6)

He has intruded upon our depraved hearts and brought us across the boundary from the world of the prince of the power of the air, in which we were willingly enslaved to sin, into his kingdom. He has set us free from sin and has seated us in the heavenly places. If God hadn't trespassed our boundaries of sinful self-will, we would have been forever doomed to the everlasting wrath of God. Ed Welch reminds us, "He (God) violates the boundaries we establish and offers forgiveness for the ones we violated."[11] Scripture teaches that God is sovereign over all things, including our wills (Ephesians 1:11; Philippians 2:13). Cloud and Townsend's assertion that God does not "nag" us could also be misunderstood. Through the prophets, God continually pleaded with his people to turn from their sin and repent: "The LORD, the God of their fathers, sent persistently to them by his messengers, because he had compassion on his people and on his dwelling place" (2 Chronicles 36:15).

Another statement which could easily be misunderstood is the statement that "Christ never takes away our will or asks us to do something hurtful. He never pushes us past our limits."[12] While it is true that we make choices for which we are responsible, Christ often asks us, his disciples, to do hard things which will hurt, at least in the short run. We are called to take up our crosses and follow him (Matthew 16:24–26)—which will involve suffering and loss. He warns that following him may cause alienation from our loved ones (Luke 12:51–53). We are told that, when we come to faith, we become "slaves of righteousness" (Romans 6:18b). The author of Hebrews challenges us, "In your struggle against sin you have not yet resisted to the point of shedding your blood" (Hebrews 12:4). Jesus pushes us beyond our limits as he calls us to do hard things that are humanly impossible.

Perhaps the most troubling statement made by the authors concerns their teaching that it can be right to be angry with God:

> In our deepest honesty and ownership of our true person there is room for expressing anger at God. Many people who are cut off from God shut down emotionally because they feel that it is not safe to tell him how angry they are at him.[13]

While it is true that believers who are suffering or experiencing loss may be tempted to be angry with God because we don't like or understand what he is doing, such anger is never encouraged or justified in Scripture. Anger involves making a judgment against wrongdoing. God is completely right and just in all that he does: "The Rock, his work is perfect, for all his ways are justice. A God of faithfulness and without iniquity, just and upright is he" (Deuteronomy 32:4).

The first recorded case of someone being angry with God was Cain, who was angry because his offering was not accepted (Genesis 4:5). Cain's anger led him to murder his brother and resulted in his banishment. Job is commended for not accusing God of wrongdoing during unfathomable suffering. When his children and property were taken from him, "in all this Job did not sin or charge God with wrong" (Job 1:22). Later, when Job experiences physical affliction, his wife encourages him to "'Curse God and die.' But he said to her, 'You speak as one of the foolish women would speak. Shall we receive good from God, and shall we not receive evil?' In all this Job did not sin with his lips" (Job 2:9–10). Later, after Job had been tempted to question

God's justice (Job 6:1–30), and after the Lord had spoken to him directly, he humbled himself before the Lord:

> Then Job answered the Lord and said: "I know that you can do all things, and that no purpose of yours can be thwarted. 'Who is this that hides counsel without knowledge?' Therefore, I have uttered what I did not understand, things too wonderful for me, which I did not know. 'Hear, and I will speak; I will question you, and you make it known to me.' I had heard of you by the hearing of the ear, but now my eye sees you; therefore, I despise myself, and repent in dust and ashes." (Job 42:1–6)

When we don't understand or like what the sovereign Lord is doing, we are called, like Job, to humble ourselves. When we are tempted to be angry because of suffering or loss, we must trust that the Lord's way is best: "Trust in the Lord with all your heart, and do not lean on your own understanding. In all your ways acknowledge him, and he will make straight your paths" (Proverbs 3:5–6).

The psalmists also wrestle with situations in which they don't understand why the Lord, who loves them, allows them to experience hardship and injustice (Psalm 73:1–14; 77:7–10). They cry out in confusion and lament, but anger toward God is never acceptable. On the cross, Jesus endured the greatest possible suffering, ultimately according to the sovereign will of the Father: "Yet it was the will of the Lord to crush him; he has put him to grief" (Isaiah 53:10a). Our Lord never expressed anger against the Father, whose purpose he was fulfilling. He did cry out (lament), "My God, my God, why have you forsaken me?" (Matthew 27:46). In the end, his suffering was turned to joy (Hebrews 12:2): "He shall see his offspring; he shall prolong his days; the will of the Lord shall prosper in his hand" (Isaiah 53:10b). In the same way, the psalmists who are suffering often find hope when they remember God's past faithfulness and look forward to his future faithfulness (Psalm 73:15–20; 77:11–15).

The positive treatment of our anger toward others is particularly troubling

While there is such a thing as righteous anger, Scripture treats most anger as a dangerous sin. The authors claim that anger is a signal that we are victims of boundary violation: "Anger tells us that our boundaries have been violated . . . telling us that we are in danger of being injured or controlled."[14] They continue, "Anger is also a signal. Like fear, anger signals danger. However, rather than urging us to withdraw anger is a sign that we need to move forward to confront the threat."[15] They also add, "Anger also provides us with a sense of power to solve a problem. It energizes us to protect ourselves, those we love, and our principles."[16] This man-centered approach ignores how most of our anger is sinful. Scripture reveals the sinful reasons which motivate our anger:

> What causes quarrels and what causes fights among you? Is it not this, that your passions are at war within you? You desire and do not have, so you murder. You covet and cannot obtain, so you fight and quarrel. You do not have, because you do not ask. (James 4:1–2)

One could argue that James 4:1–2 states that we get angry because our boundaries have been violated—others didn't treat us the way we wanted them to—but such anger, according to James, is not justified but murderous.

Cloud and Townsend use the example of Jesus confronting the merchants in the temple as an example of righteous anger over violated boundaries. The problem with their interpretation is that Jesus's passion was not for the violation of his personal boundaries but rather it was zeal for his Father's house which moved him to clear the temple (John 2:13–17).

This positive spin on anger is dangerous. It is what our sinful flesh wants to hear. We want to justify ourselves and to express our anger by judging others. But James warns that, contrary to our expectations and desires, "the anger of man does not produce the righteousness of God" (James 1:20). Jesus warned that anger can be murderous and can subject us to God's judgment (Matthew 5:21–22). There are many other warnings in Scripture against the destructive power of sinful anger (Proverbs 25:28; Galatians 5:20–21; Colossians 3:8). I am deeply concerned that this unbalanced teaching could be used by many to excuse sinful anger, thus giving the devil an opportunity (Ephesians 4:26–27). Scripture offers a wiser approach to our anger: "Good sense makes one slow to anger, and it is his glory to overlook an offense" (Proverbs 19:11).

In summary, while Cloud and Townsend identify a real and common problem for many Christians, their approach focuses too much on setting boundaries for self-protection in our horizontal relationships with others. Instead, we should set priorities and limits with a vertical focus striving to determine from Scripture how we can best love God and neighbor. Don't go from pleasing others to pleasing self. Instead, please God.

ENDNOTES

Chapter 1

1. Richard Rodgers and Oscar Hammerstein II, "I'm Just a Girl Who Cain't Say No," in *Oklahoma!* (New York: Random House, 1943), act 1, scene 1. Lyrics by Oscar Hammerstein II, music by Richard Rodgers. First performed on March 31, 1943, at the St. James Theatre, New York.

2. Karl Pillemer, *Fault Lines: Fractured Families and How to Mend Them* (Avery, 2020), p. 5, cited in Abigail Shrier, *Bad Therapy: Why the Kids Aren't Growing Up* (Sentinel, 2024), 60.

3. Henry Cloud and John Townsend, *Boundaries: When to Say Yes, How to Say No to Take Control of Your Life* (Zondervan, 2017).

4. Edward T. Welch, "Boundaries in Relationships," *The Journal of Biblical Counseling* 22, no. 3 (Spring 2004), 20.

Chapter 6

1. Abigail Shrier, *Bad Therapy: Why the Kids Aren't Growing Up* (Sentinel, 2024), 61.

2. Jim Newheiser, *Parenting Is More Than a Formula* (P&R Publishing, 2015); Elyse Fitzpatrick, Jim Newheiser, and Laura Hendrickson, *When Good Kids Make Bad Choices: Help and Hope for Hurting Parents* (Harvest House Publishers, 2005); Jim Newheiser and Elyse Fitzpatrick, *You Never Stop Being a Parent: Thriving in Relationship with Your Adult Children* (P&R Publishing, 2010).

Chapter 7

1. Heath Lambert, *Finally Free: Fighting for Purity with the Power of Grace* (Zondervan, 2013).

2. Tim Keller and Kathy Keller, *The Meaning of Marriage: Facing the Complexities of Commitment with the Wisdom of God* (Penguin, 2011), 267–68.

3. Keller and Keller, *The Meaning of Marriage*, 268.

4. Keller and Keller, *The Meaning of Marriage*, 257.

Chapter 8

1. Reasons for not reporting the abuse could be because of the nature of the allegations, the lack of proof, and the time that had passed. I realize that some would say that her brother should be reported and exposed for the sake of other potential victims (Matthew 7:12). Another consideration would be whether any particular children were in danger of being abused by this man.

Chapter 9

1. Jim Newheiser, *Money: Seeking God's Wisdom*, 31-Day Devotionals for Life (P&R Publishing, 2019).

Chapter 11

1. David Rosenberg and Natalia Szura, "Teens are spending the equivalent of a 40-hour work week on their devices. Here's how to help them find the right balance," Fortune Well, October 24, 2023, https://fortune.com/well/2023/10/24/teens-too-much-screen-time-find-balance/.

2. Beata Mostafavi, "Study: Average Teen Received More Than 200 App Notifications A Day," Michigan Medicine, September 26, 2023, https://www.michiganmedicine.org/health-lab/study-average-teen-received-more-200-app-notifications-day.

3. Jonathan Haidt, *The Anxious Generation: How the Great Rewiring of Childhood is Causing an Epidemic of Mental Illness* (Penguin Random House, 2024).

4. Cloud and Townsend, *Boundaries,* 219–29.

5. See more at https://www.anxiousgeneration.com/take-action.

Appendix

1. Henry Cloud and John Townsend, *Boundaries: When to Say Yes, How to Say No to Take Control of Your Life* (Zondervan, 2017), 29.

2. Cloud and Townsend, *Boundaries*, 136.

3. Edward T. Welch, "Boundaries in Relationships," *The Journal of Biblical Counseling* 22, no. 3 (Spring 2004), 16.

4. Cloud and Townsend, *Boundaries*, 33.

5. Cloud and Townsend, *Boundaries*, 49.

6. Cloud and Townsend, *Boundaries*, 296.

7. Cloud and Townsend, *Boundaries*, 307.

8. Cloud and Townsend, *Boundaries*, 305.

9. Cloud and Townsend, *Boundaries,* 259–66.

10. Cloud and Townsend, *Boundaries*, 260.

11. Welch, "Boundaries in Relationships," 17.

12. Cloud and Townsend, *Boundaries*, 164.

13. Cloud and Townsend, *Boundaries*, 261.

14. Cloud and Townsend, *Boundaries*, 114.

15. Cloud and Townsend, *Boundaries*, 114.

16. Cloud and Townsend, *Boundaries*, 114.